# Volume 1: Beware of the New Apostolic Reformation

A Sound Word Ministry Publication

# Beware of the New Apostolic Reformation!

A Movement of Counterfeit Spirituality
Globally Infiltrating Biblical Christianity

© May, 2020
Sound Word Ministry
*"A light in the post-modern darkness"*
1st printing --, October, 2015
2nd printing -- February, 2016
3rd printing -- June, 2016
4th printing – September, 2016
5th printing – June, 2017
6th printing - September, 2018
7th printing - May, 2020
ISBN # 978-1-64871-559-4

Unless specified, "Scriptures taken from the NEW AMERICAN STANDARD BIBLE, Copyright 1960, 1962, 1963, 1968, 1971, 1973, 1975, 1977, 1995. by the Lockman Foundation. Used by permission."

**Many thanks to Robert H.** for the sheep cover illustration and help with editing, formatting, and layout. Used by permission.

**Copyright Disclaimer.** Under Section 107 of the Copyright Act of 1976, allowance is made for fair use for purposes such as criticism, comment, news reporting, teaching, scholarship, and research.

More copies of this booklet, along with our newer one, A Hidden Path, Bethel Redding and Beyond are available on Amazon.

Please see our website @ soundwordministry.org for more helpful information and resources.

Authors can be reached at–soundwordministry1@gmail.com

*You will know the truth and the truth will set you free.* All praise and glory goes to Jesus Christ alone who is the only Way, the only Truth, and the only Life. Amen.

# TABLE OF CONTENTS

## VOLUME 1 – Beware of the New Apostolic Reformation!

I. What is the New Apostolic Reformation?---------------------------------5

II. Dominion Theology-----------------------------------------------------------9

III. False Doctrines---------------------------------------------------------------10

IV. Restoration of "Apostles" and "Prophets"-----------------------------18

V. Occult and New Age Emphasis-------------------------------------------21

VI. Strategic Level Spiritual Warfare----------------------------------------26

VIII. Conclusion-------------------------------------------------------------------30

# I. <u>What is the New Apostolic Reformation</u>?

Founded by Dr. C. Peter Wagner, it is made up of thousands of networks of churches and ministries around the world that share core beliefs and a common agenda. "Apostles" and "prophets" lead the movement with ongoing "new revelation" that they believe is needed to fulfill their God-given mandate to establish a physical kingdom of God on earth. In her book, *The Reformation Manifesto*, Cindy Jacobs, co-founder of Generals International and leader of NAR's Reformation Prayer Network claims—

> *When Jesus came to earth, He wasn't only looking for converts. He was looking to re-create heaven on earth.*[1]

One of their main beliefs is that a paradigm shift occurred in 2001 when the primary commission of the church changed from souls to transforming society and from the discipling of individuals to the discipling of nations. C. Peter Wagner states—

> *Revival is not enough. We need a paradigm shift.*[2]

> *We began by over-identifying the church with the kingdom and going on from there to imagine that our mission was to save souls and plant churches and let others worry about improving society. No longer!* [Cindy] *Jacobs is proclaiming a "reformation manifesto".*[3]

Dr. Wagner also shares about the enormity of the movement and its radical differences:

> *The New Apostolic Reformation is growing faster than Islam. It is important to recognize that we are not talking about something on the fringes, but about a dynamic movement at the very heart of 21st century Christianity.*[4]

> *The New Apostolic Reformation is an extraordinary work of God that is changing the shape of Protestant Christianity around the world.*[5]

> *Many Christian leaders still have no idea that this NAR movement even exists. However, some have stereotypes that relegate the movement to the lunatic fringe of Christianity. The movement is even threatening to some because of the radical differences in style in contrast to the traditional churches most of us have known.*[6]

The roots of NAR go back further; however, as an almost, identical agenda was presented in the 1940's through the New Order of the Latter Rain (NOLR) movement.

In 1946, a revival began in San Diego, CA under the leadership of Franklin Hall. Hall believed that Christians can become immortal through different stages of spiritual growth as outlined in his book, *The Return of Immortality.* The subject of immortality greatly influenced many others who also embraced Hall's teaching. Shortly thereafter, the Sharon Home revival rose up in North Battlefield, Saskatchewan, Canada, led by George Hawtin, Ern Baxter, and George Warnock. Warnock's book, *The Feast of the Tabernacles*, laid out the doctrines for the New Order of the Latter Rain—including the perfection of the saints and their dominion over the earth.

At the same time, a former Baptist minister, William Branham, was holding forth miracle services with many people spectacularly healed and delivered in the name of Jesus Christ—although he credited the signs and wonders to his angel whom he believed was the one who performed them. Unfortunately, what seemed like the most dynamic, supernatural ministry that the church had ever seen, came Branham's false teachings such as— (1) the Trinity and church denominations are of the devil, (2) the three forms of God's Word are: the Bible, the Zodiac, and the Egyptian pyramids, (3) his "Serpent Seed" doctrine which suggests that the serpent in the Garden had sexual intimacy with Eve that resulted in the conception of Cain, (4) His angel who taught him that he (Branham) was Elijah before the $2^{nd}$ coming as well as being the messenger of the last church age, Laodicea, and (5) believers would reach immortality before Christ returns—and become a super race (also known as Joel's Army) (see page 15).

William Branham is known as the father of the Latter Rain movement, the influence of whom many in the charismatic/Pentecostal churches are still operating in today—especially the beliefs that certain lost truths are being restored, and that God gives new revelation through supernatural encounters with angels and through visions. Often, these experiences and new interpretations of scripture were placed above the Scriptures— which they believe was needed to equip and prepare the body of Christ for the next "move of God."

Other beliefs of the New Order of the Latter Rain were—(1) the restoration of the church and the offices of apostles and prophets, (2) the restoration of the Tabernacle of David, (3) the expectation of a huge end-times revival, and (4) the Manifestation of the Sons of God doctrine (see page 15). The New Order of the Latter Rain movement quickly appeared to have died out in 1949, much because the Assemblies of God took a strong stand and renounced their doctrines as heresy at that time:

> *RESOLVED, that we disapprove of those extreme teachings and practices, which, being unfounded scripturally, serve only to break fellowship of like precious faith and tend to confusion and division among the members of the body of Christ, and be it hereby known that this 23rd General Council disapproves of the so-called "New Order of the Latter Rain."*

Dr. C. Peter Wagner does not agree. In his autobiography, *Wrestling with Alligators, Prophets, and Theologians,* he wrote this about the Latter Rain movement:

> *They were pioneers. They were risk-takers. Their positive contributions to God's kingdom far overshadowed any mistakes they might have made.*[7]

During the 1990's, the agenda of the New Order of the Latter Rain revisited the church once again but with another name—The New Apostolic Reformation.

As you will see in the following pages of this book, the New Apostolic Reformation prophets, leaders and teachers speak repeatedly about such things as: mysticism, transformation, reformation, paradigm shift, new breed, etc. Their definitions of these words share common beliefs with the New Age movement as described in Warren Smith's book, *False Christ Coming, Does Anybody Care?*

Smith provides the following information about messages received by Maitreya (the awaited New Age Messiah) that were channeled (spoken through) New Age practitioners such as: Alice Bailey, Marianne Williamson, and Benjamin Crème. The messages that were channeled are almost identical to what is spoken about today through the "prophets" of NAR. Some examples of these channeled messages are as follows:

Transformation:

> *Share with me, my friends, in a Great Work, nothing less than the **transformation** of the world.*[8]

Reformation:

> *The Master Jesus is going to **reform** the Christian churches.*[9]

New Revelation:

> *The Christian faith also has served its purpose; its Founder seeks to bring a **new gospel** and a **new message** that will enlighten all men everywhere.*[10]

Mysticism:

> *It is a **mystical** revolution that will usher in a **mystical** age.*[11]

Paradigm shift:

> *But this **paradigm shift** will take great wisdom, great courage, and massive determination...*[12]

Experience over doctrine:

> *Therefore, in the new world order, spirituality will supersede theology; living **experience** will take the place of theological acceptances.*[13]

> *I do not want you to believe in me, or not to believe in me, I want you to **experience** me.*[14]

New Breed:

> *The New Agers believe that through meditation and other "spiritual disciplines" that they have become a **"new species"**...*[15]

Little gods:

> *The significance of incarnation and resurrection is not that Jesus was a human like us—but rather that **we are gods** like him—or at least we have the potential to be. The*

> *significance of Jesus is not as a vehicle of salvation but as a model of perfection.* [16]

## II. Dominion Theology

Dominionists believe that God has given the church a mandate, under the leadership of their "apostles" and "prophets," to— 1) bring the kingdom of heaven down to earth, (2) establish a one, unified, global church that will transform society and, (3) take dominion over the earth. Their unusual interpretation of Genesis 1:26 is extreme because it includes the dominion of human society which was not God's original plan. C. Peter Wagner writes about church dominion:

> *. . .we have an assignment from God to take dominion and transform society.* [17]

> *Little did I imagine that in the same year of 2001, I would take the first steps into what I now consider to be the most radical, and potentially world-changing paradigm shift of all, namely, understanding and applying God's dominion mandate.* [18]

This is the dominion mandate simply stated: God created Adam to have dominion over the earth. Satan usurped man's dominion through the fall in the Garden of Eden. God wants to use the church to take dominion back from Satan. The church now has a mandate from God to rule over all earthly governments and institutions. Jesus **cannot and will not** return until this happens.

On the website, *My Word Like Fire*, Cindy Jacobs is quoted as follows:

> *Because we didn't understand our commission, sin came into the world and it began to deteriorate the ability we had to steward the earth. So we have authority to reverse the Genesis curse of poverty and death. Not only do we have the power to do so—we have the mandate. You have to understand this.*

> *And God showed me that every part of the Lord's Prayer is an element on how to reform and transform a nation.*

C. Peter Wagner also says this about Dominionism:

> *Jesus, having won back authority on earth, could now mediate and rule in the affairs of earth. However, Jesus did not stay on the earth to rule it. He ascended to the Father and is seated at His right hand. So who is now responsible to rule and reign in the earth? Believe it or not, the church, which is the body of Christ.*[19]

In his book, *the Seven Mountains Prophecy*, Johnny Enlow, adds—

> *In essence, the Father says to the Son, 'Once You have purchased redemption for mankind, You will sit at my right hand... You will remain up here as the head, and Your body on earth will crush your enemies. Until they do so, You are not going back to rescue, rapture, save, or anything else. Your body, in fact, will not be a beautiful bride until she has accomplished this crushing of Satan.*[20]

**My Kingdom is not of this world.** John 18:36

It is interesting to note that most leaders and pastors who are in the NAR will deny being a dominionist or having any involvement in the movement at all when asked. As a result, the majority of believers who attend these churches and conferences have no awareness of the huge networks being formed around them. Few have even heard of the "NAR"—the New Apostolic Reformation.

## III. False Doctrines

Dominionism isn't the only false doctrine that followers of the New Apostolic Reformation believe. The following is a very brief summary of some of the other false doctrines connected to NAR in some way.

**1. Kenosis**—the belief that Jesus came as a man, did His miracles as a man and had to **achieve** his divinity—and so can we. Bill Johnson, senior pastor of Bethel Church in Redding, CA says this about who Jesus is—

> *Jesus Christ said of Himself, "The Son can do nothing."... He had NO supernatural capabilities whatsoever! While He is 100 percent God, He chose to live with the same limitations that man would face once He was redeemed. He made that point over and over again. Jesus became the model for all who would embrace*

*the invitation to invade the impossible in His name. He performed miracles, wonders, and signs, as a man in right relationship to God . . . not as God. If He performed miracles because He was God, then they would be unattainable for us. But if He did them as a man, I am responsible to pursue His lifestyle. Recapturing this simple truth changes everything . . . and makes possible a full restoration of the ministry of Jesus in His Church.*[21]

What we believe about the divinity of Jesus Christ is at the very core of a Christian believer's faith. To say that "Jesus did miracles as a man in right relationship with God because He was setting a model for us to follow" minimizes the divinity of Jesus and elevates us as human beings.

**2. Healing and Prosperity**—Many NAR leaders teach what is known as the Prosperity Gospel which is also known as "name it and claim it" Word of Faith theology. They believe that—

(1) **Our faith is a force** and that our words are carriers of that force.

(2) **Positive confession**—believers can cause to happen what they say with their words. The Law of Attraction is the belief that if we confess positively about something, good things will come to us. But, on the other hand, if we think or speak negatively, we can curse ourselves and bad things will come to us.

(3) **Decreeing and Declaring**—NAR followers believe that all you need to get what you want from God is to attach the phrase "I decree and declare" in front of a prayer and God is obligated to answer that prayer.

(4) **Jesus is Perfect Theology**—Bill Johnson teaches that everything we say and do should be seen and heard in the life of Jesus during the three and a half years that He walked on the earth because He alone is "perfect theology." Bill Johnson teaches that people should never be sick. He also teaches that Jesus heals every time.

> *I refuse to create a theology that allows for sickness. Paul refers to his thorn in the flesh which has been interpreted as disease allowed or brought on by God. That is a*

> *different gospel. Jesus didn't model it and He didn't teach it. You have a false gospel if you don't teach that Jesus heals every time – always intends healing every time.*[22]

Yet Paul tells us in Galatians – the opposite—

> ***I beg of you, brethren, become as I am, for I also have become as you are. You have done me no wrong; but you know that it was because of a bodily illness that I preached the gospel to you the first time; and that which was a trial to you in my bodily condition you did not despise or loathe, but you received me as an angel of God, as Christ Jesus Himself.*** Gal.4:12-14

Many teach that **if we are sick, it is our fault;** and/or if we ask God to heal us and we remain sick, it is because we don't have enough faith, haven't done enough spiritual warfare, or haven't decreed and declared enough. The same applies to wealth and prosperity. But in the case of wealth and prosperity—it's because we haven't tithed enough!

We know that Christ healed every manner of sickness and disease—and that He still heals today. It is also true that we have power in His Name, and we need to passionately pray for the sick, and make our requests known to God. But the Bible gives no formulas for healing, makes no guarantees, nor mentions anything about positive confession, decreeing and declaring, or claiming a healing.

**3. Extra-biblical Revelation and Experiencing God**—Leaders of the New Apostolic Reformation teach about the importance of reading the Bible but, at the same time, teach about the importance of extra-biblical revelation knowledge.

Revelation knowledge can be attained by words spoken through prophesy, trips to heaven, contemplative prayer, visions, and trances to name a few ways. These venues used are dangerous because many of them require altered states of consciousness of some sort, and they leave one vulnerable to a false spirit, a false Jesus, and/or false doctrines.

Johnson says this in his book, When Heaven Invades Earth—

> . . .*Those who feel safe because of their intellectual grasp of Scriptures enjoy a false sense of security. None of us has a full grasp of Scripture, but we all have the Holy Spirit. He is our common denominator who will always lead us into truth. But to follow Him, we must be willing to follow off the map—to go beyond what we know. To do so successfully we must recognize His presence above all.*[23]

He continues in his same book by saying this—

> *Jesus did not say, "My sheep will know my book." It is His voice that we are to know. Why the distinction? Because anyone can know the Bible as a book—the devil himself knows and quotes the Scriptures. But only those whose lives are dependent on the person of the Holy Spirit will consistently recognize His voice.*[24]

Yet the following is what we learn in the Word of God—

> **All Scripture is inspired by God and profitable for teaching, for reproof, for correction, for training in righteousness;**
>
> **So that the man of God may be adequate, equipped for <u>every</u> good work. 2 Timothy 3:16-17**

The need for more revelation contained in the NAR belief system diminishes the power and truth of the Scriptures in favor of a personal encounter and extra-biblical revelation—assumed to be received from the true Holy Spirit. Assumption is especially dangerous in light of the fact that nearly all cults and false religions were founded upon the premise that some angel or voice spoke to a willing participant who received a "new doctrine" or "new revelation," and then started a new religion or movement.

**4. Manifestation of the Sons of God**— The most radical belief connected with the New Apostolic Reformation is the "Manifestation of the Sons of God" (MSOG) doctrine. This is not a new teaching at all but a common theme among cults and various fringe groups throughout the centuries. Although its modern roots stem from the New Order of the

Latter Rain movement, it was also voiced through the "prophetic" revelations of Jane Leade, a 17$^{th}$ century mystic.

Some prophesy that there will be a second Pentecost when God will manifest Himself through a select, elite, many-membered, remnant body and give them more supernatural power than the believers experienced in the early church. Some also believe that they will continue to receive more and more of God's power until they become "manifest" as sons of God, a "new breed" (also known as Joel's Army or Overcomers)—one in nature and in essence with Christ—so much so that they will have the ability to defeat death itself (immortalization) **BEFORE** the return of Christ. Dr. Bill Hamon says this:

> *A greater measure of revelation, faith, and overcoming grace is being released in the Church. The mortal Church is in transition and in preparation for becoming the immortal Church. The resurrection-translation of the saints that brings about the redemption of their bodies into immortal, indestructible bodies will take place so that God can fulfill His greater purpose for and through His Church. There is a last day ministry designed for the overcoming Church to accomplish in the heavenlies and on earth that will require the saints to have their bodies redeemed.*[25]

How they believe this 2$^{nd}$ Pentecost will happen is that this remnant church will become a corporate, "second Mary." Some teach that when the Shekinah Glory comes in the form of a cloud and overshadows this remnant Church with the passion of a bridegroom (Luke 1:35, 9:34), this elite group will be impregnated with the Holy Spirit and the corporate Christ within her will be incarnated ("God in the flesh"). They refer to this conception as the "manchild" referred to in Revelation 12:5 (King James version)

The actual Greek translation for the word "manchild" is "male child." Most Christians believe that the "male" child" is Jesus at his birth. But Lance Wallnau describes the "male child" differently in a video he posted on his Facebook page on December 25, 2015, entitled "Christmas Word."

> *Why is it called a manchild? Because it is not a baby wrapped in swaddling clothes. It is an adult in the infancy of a final metamorphosis of revival. Let me say that again. A manchild is a full-grown baby meaning it's going to be adults that are stepping into the infancy of the first phase of the final move of God. So it*

> *is a child but it is a man. It's the body of Christ stepping into its final act and this company is made up of overcomers but—not everybody is there.*

Lance Wallnau goes on in this same video to explain who this male child is:

> *This child is caught up to the throne so we have to continue to press into the realm of the prophetic, the supernatural, soaking, and intercession. We have to keep going, folks, into this revelation. We have to learn how to go up and in, up and into the realm of the presence of God because ultimately this company is going to be taken to the third heaven and I don't think they are taken to a place where they are unfamiliar."* [He is referring to those in the church who are currently "visiting heaven" and having encounters there, yet he does not cite any scripture to support this statement. See p. 12].

Francis Frangipane, author and founding pastor of River of Life Ministries says it this way:

> *Even now, hell trembles and the heavens watch in awe. For I say to you, once again, the 'virgin is with child'. Before Jesus Himself returns, the last virgin Church shall become pregnant with the promise of God. Out of her travail, the body of Christ shall come forth, raised to the full stature of its head, the Lord Jesus. Corporately manifested in holiness, power and love, the Bride of Christ shall arise clothed in white garments, bright and clean.*[49]
>
> *Indeed, our purity, our spiritual virginity as the body of Christ, is nothing less than God preparing us as He did Mary to 'give birth' to the ministry of His Son. Even now the spiritual womb of the virgin church, the holy purpose of Christ is growing, awaiting maturity; ready to be born in power in the timing of God.*[27]

We believe that Christian believers cannot achieve any change through special anointings, impartation, warfare, or any other way. The following scripture tells us that we will receive our glorified bodies **from Jesus Christ Himself** when He returns.

> ***Behold, I tell you a mystery; we will not all sleep, but we will all be changed, in a moment, in the***

> *twinkling of an eye, at the last trumpet; for the trumpet will sound, and the dead will be raised imperishable, AND WE WILL BE CHANGED. I Cor. 15:51. See also II Tim. 4:3-5*

Another part of this doctrine is that an army of believers led by the NAR "apostles" and "prophets" will execute judgment before the return of the Lord—as they believe in a need to restore the earth—in order for Jesus Christ to return for a perfect body. Dr. Bill Hamon presents this about restoration and his unusual interpretation of Acts 3:21.

> *Acts 3:21 emphatically declares that Jesus cannot be released from heaven to come back to earth until all things are restored by the Church. If Christ Jesus has not returned, then that means there is more restoration that must take place. The moment the last thing is restored, then Christ will return.*[28]

Church leaders today vary about their beliefs concerning the rapture of the church. Some have traditional beliefs, yet others teach that there will be no need for a rapture of the Church. They believe this because—when all people-groups and governments of this world are submitted to the NAR, they not only rid the earth of demons but also eliminate all "systemic poverty", Christ will return to a glorious kingdom paradise on earth accomplished by his perfect Church who will hand Him the Kingdom. They believe that Jesus **cannot** and **will not return** until this is finished—the Kingdom of heaven brought down to earth.

Rick Joyner shares his beliefs about the Rapture of the church:

> *The doctrine of the Rapture was a great and effective ruse of the enemy to implant in the church a retreat mentality ... already this yoke has been cast off by the majority in the advancing church and it will soon be cast off by all.*[29]

Dr. Bill Hamon adds—

> *If evangelical and charismatic Christians would get as excited about growing up as they do about going up, the body of Christ would reach its maturity much sooner, fulfill all Scriptures, restore all things, and thereby "bring back King Jesus".*[30]

> *For the Lord Himself will descend from heaven with a shout, with the voice of the archangel and with the trumpet of God, and the dead in Christ will rise first. Then we who are alive and remain will be caught up together with them in the clouds to meet the Lord in the air, and so we shall be with the Lord. I Thess. 4:16-18*

In addition, C. Peter Wagner in his book, *Dominion*, offers his aberrant views about the end times:

> ". . . but none of the signs of Matthew 24:4-34 are expected to precede His return, because they have already occurred."[31] [Wagner admits that he is a Preterist—one who believes the false teaching that the tribulation already happened in 70 A.D.—even though most scholars agree that the Book of Revelation was not written until approximately 90 A.D.]

As the updated version of this book goes to print, the entire world is faced with the Covid-19, global pandemic with thousands of people losing their lives daily. There was not a peep from their so-called prophets warning the body of Christ about the Coronavirus. In fact, some of their "prophets," after the virus spread globally, gave false predictions about when the pandemic would end. Yet many will forget about these predictions and will continue to blindly follow." This is what Wagner said about how the condition of the world would keep getting better and better--

> *We no longer accept the idea that society will get worse and worse because we now believe that God's mandate is to transform society so that it gets better and better.*[32] [Scripture clearly teaches that this world will continue to get worse as we move into the last days. In fact, Jesus tells us that events getting worse is a **very** sign that He's coming back soon— and that we should **"look up" not take over]!**

Instead of the focus being the blessed hope for the return of Jesus Christ to rapture his church—which was the belief that was shared by the original apostles and Christians throughout the centuries—rather, the focus of the New Apostolic Reformation has shifted to the glorification of

*In a nutshell*

the Church to redeem society. Dr. Bill Hamon tells us this about the full maturity and the responsibility of the church:

> *The earth and all of creation are waiting for the manifestation of the sons of God, the time when they will come into their maturity and immortalization... The Church has a responsibility and ministry to the rest of creation. Earth and its natural creation is anxiously waiting for the Church to reach full maturity and come to full son-ship. When the Church realizes its full son-ship, its bodily redemption will cause a redemptive chain reaction throughout all of creation.*[33]

## IV. Restoration of Apostles and Prophets

NAR leaders believe in the restoration of "apostles" who will hold the highest position of government in the church. They teach that ALL believers, local churches, and each city must submit to an "apostle" who will rule over their designated region. They also believe that only through these apostles will the church have the ability to fulfill its destiny. C. Peter Wagner describes the importance and necessity of "apostles" in the church:

> *Apostolic networks replace denominations.*[34]

> *They [pastors] are convinced that they would not be able to reach their full destiny in serving God apart from the spiritual covering of the apostle.*[35]

> *When the apostles begin to rise by the thousands, we will be able to take the nations for Jesus Christ. The harvest cannot be brought in apart from this foundational office. If [John Kelly] is right, the apostolic office is so important that it can mean the difference between heaven and hell for multitudes.*[36]

Dr. Bill Hamon, a member of NAR's Apostolic Council of Prophetic Elders, adds—

> *It is almost impossible for individuals to humble themselves under God without humbling themselves in submission and relationship to Christ's delegated representatives [apostles] of Him to His church.*[37]

They believe that the apostles and prophets of the New Apostolic Reformation are the ones who hear from God in regard to the affairs of the church. Dr. Bill Hamon warns about the need to be submitted to the apostles' authority:

> *Learn to recognize the true voice of God through His holy apostles and prophets.*[38]
>
> *You are not in divine order unless you are an apostle or under one.*[39]
>
> *The choice is ours to submit, believe, and become one with the whole body of Christ or to rebel, refuse, stiffen our necks, and be devoured.*[40]

C. Peter Wagner adds—

> *Contrary to what some people might think, however, it is not the responsibility of all believers, nor even of church pastors, to hear directly what the Spirit is saying to the churches. Apostles are the ones who have been given the primary responsibility of hearing what the Spirit is saying to the churches.*[41]

> **For such men are false apostles, deceitful workers, disguising themselves as apostles of Christ. No wonder, for even Satan disguises himself as an angel of light.** II Cor. 11:13-15

They believe in the restoration of the office of the prophet in the church—yet their leaders confess that the words of their prophets are not 100% accurate. In fact, many of the "prophesies" given prove to be false and/or vague.

Even Mike Bickel, well known director of International House of Prayer (IHOP), a ministry that "trains" people in the prophetic ministry, admits that most visions, prophesies, and visitations are not from God:

> *I get, I don't know how many dreams and visions sent to me because of the internet around the world, email, and from members of IHOP. Most of them I don't pay attention to. I think they are a distraction. They are not real. I don't mean the people aren't real. Some of them are faking it and there are a lot of people faking it. But even good people just have dumb stuff – it's just dumb stuff. Probably 80% of what I hear I throw away. It doesn't move me at all. It doesn't bear witness to me. I still like the guy. I still believe in his walk with God but I don't believe what he says is from God.*[42]

Yet, Bill Hamon goes so far as to say this about the modern day prophets of the New Apostolic Reformation:

> *God is very sensitive about His prophets. To touch one of His prophets is to touch the apple of His eye. To reject God's prophets is to reject God. To fail to recognize the prophets, or to keep them from speaking, is to refuse God permission to speak.*[43]

Moreover, they believe their prophets receive direct insight from God regarding new revelation and application of the Scriptures. If one questions a NAR prophet or pastor about what is said, he is often: (1) treated hostilely, (2) labeled: "divisive", "rebellious", a "Jezebel", "not spiritually mature enough to understand" and/or, (3) shunned by the congregation.

In light of the fact that most false religions and cults are rooted in an individual claiming to receive direct revelation from angels or a supernatural encounter of some sort, it is vital that we be like the Bereans and "examine all things carefully." It is also important and scriptural to have the freedom to ask questions to church leaders without reproach.

Furthermore, their "prophetic" words proclaim the strategies and new ideas confirming their agenda which they believe prepares the body of Christ for the next step within the movement.

Johnny Enlow "prophesied" on the *The Elijah List* (a popular, NAR respected internet website) that angels will soon offer scrolls that will reveal secrets regarding God's new reformation:

> *A very elite prayer force has been prepared in refining fire and now new fuel will come on prayer gatherings. An angelic company will also be releasing scrolls to the prayer movement leaders, and it will cause a season of praying effective and effectual prayers, as hidden secrets from God are released regarding His reformation agenda.*[44]

> **Many false prophets will arise and will mislead many. . . . *if possible even the elect.*** Matt. 24:11. Also Jer. 23:16-40, Eze. 13:1-10, Deut. 13 & 18

They believe that God has revealed to them the strategy of the Seven Mountains Mandate as a way to penetrate, influence and dominate the institutions of—family, government, education, arts/entertainment, media, business, and religion, and the Seven Mountains Mandate is a means to achieve their dominion goals. They also believe that when the church achieves this goal and sets up the kingdom here on earth—Jesus can return. C. Peter Wagner explains:

> *Think of the seven mountains. Satan has succeeded in maintaining control in most of them because he has established a government in each one. Furthermore, it takes a government to overthrow a government.*[45]

Jesus tells us we are salt and light in a dark world and the Apostle Paul tells us to submit to governmental authorities—not to overthrow them! **The church's mandate is not political domination but to preach the Gospel!**

## V. Occult and New Age Emphasis

NAR followers strongly emphasize the importance of experiences with angels, demons, visions, hidden/esoteric knowledge (Gnosis), traveling through portals and gates into the third heaven (astral travel) , telepathy, contemplative prayer, and quantum mysticism, Schools are offered to "train" people how to prophesy, have visions and trances, and experience (astral) soul travel through dimensions, for example.

Some church leaders glorify New Age practitioners (1) because these leaders believe that New Agers have more extensive knowledge than most Christians, and (2) because the church needs to "take back" what has been stolen and held captive by the occult/New Age. C. Peter Wagner says this:

> *I suggest that it may be possible to receive selected, but valid information from the world of darkness itself. Certain people such as shamans, witch doctors, practitioners of Eastern religions, New Age gurus or professors of the occult on university faculties are examples of the kind of people who may have much more extensive knowledge of the spirit world than most Christians have. Some of the information they furnish is accurate. Many of them are not only intelligent, but they are also sincere people of integrity.*[46]

In the book, *Physics of Heaven*, Bill Johnson shares his beliefs:

> Many prominent pastors and conference speakers add fuel to the fire of fear by assuming that because the New Age promotes it, its origins must be from the devil. I find that form of reasoning weak at best. If we follow that line of thought, we will continue to give the devil the tools that God has given us for success in life and ministry.[47]

Jonathan Welton adds:

> I have found throughout Scripture at least 75 examples of things that the New Age has counterfeited, such as: having a spirit guide, trances, meditation, auras, power objects, clairvoyance, clairaudience, and more. These actually belong to the church, but they have been stolen and cleverly repackaged.[48]

Larry Randolph continues:

> However, I suspect that many have a fear of being deceived by things they might not understand. Like Israel in the Old Testament, they are quick to relinquish anything that appears different or "spooky" in the spirit realm—to the hands of the Philistines. In which case we need the spirit of David to rise up within us and declare, "I'm taking back what belongs to God!"[49]

Is it a "spirit of David' that we need, or is it discernment? Former New Ager, Warren Smith, shares his insights about "testing the spirits":

> Today, it is very sad to see so many believers falling under the influence of the same spirit that influenced me when I was in the New Age. This spirit says that it is a time for "breakthroughs" and for the fulfillment of our "destiny"—that there is something "new" and exciting in the wind. This teaching claims that we are in the midst of a great transition that will result in a "paradigm shift," and that through <u>"new revelation" and "personal experience", God is in the process of taking the church to a "new dimension" and to a whole "new level." Many Christian leaders these days are so sure that what they are hearing and experiencing is from God, they are rarely testing the spirits, or even considering the possibility that they are being deceived.</u>[50]

The Apostle Paul had zero tolerance for false teachers, and he warns us about extra-biblical revelation that is contrary to what we learned from him:

> ***But even if we, or an angel from heaven, should preach to you a gospel contrary to what we have preached to you, he is to be accursed! As we have said before, so I say again now, if any man is preaching to you a gospel contrary to what you received, he is to be accursed!*** Galatians 1:8-9
>
> ***So then brethren stand firm and hold to the traditions which you were taught.*** II Thess. 2:15
>
> ***But I am afraid that, as the serpent deceived Eve by his craftiness, your minds will be led astray from the simplicity and purity of devotion to Christ.*** II Corinthians 11:3

Dead saints of the past cannot be complete until present-day Christians "fulfill their destiny" is another New Age teaching in the church today. Bill Johnson, pastor of Bethel Church, Redding, CA says this:

> *I believe it's possible for us to recover realms of anointing, realms of insight, realms of God, that have been untended for decades—simply by choosing to reclaim them and perpetuate them for future generations.* [51]
>
> *God is saying, "There are things that are lying there, mysteries to be understood, inheritances that are untended, uncared for, unoccupied. But they're there for the taking.* [52]

Dr. Bill Hamon adds this:

> *All of those who have died in the faith since the beginning of time are cheering us on from the balcony of heaven. They cannot be complete without the full obedience of the last-generation Church. . . the spirits of just saints have been made perfect but are waiting for their final act of redemption. But they cannot receive it until we, the last generation Church, fulfill our destiny.* [53]
>
> ***Every good thing given and every good and perfect gift is from above, coming down from the Father of***

> *lights, with whom there is no variation or shifting shadow.* James 1:17
>
> *These things I have written to you concerning those who are trying to deceive you. As for you, the anointing which you received from Him abides in you, and you have no need for anyone to teach you; but as His anointing teaches you about all things, and is true and is not a lie. .* I John 2:26-27. Also I Cor. 12:11, and II Corinthians 1:21

Other leaders even believe that there are "anointings" and "mantles" that have not been claimed from prior generations which can be obtained by lying on graves of famous, dead faith-healers (this practice is called "grave sucking"). Benny Hinn describes his experiences at the gravesites of Aimee Semple McPherson and Kathryn Kuhlman:

> *I felt a terrific anointing when I was there. I actually, I—I, hear this, I trembled when I visited Aimee's tomb. I was shaking all over. God's power came all over me. ... I believe the anointing has lingered over Aimee's body. I know this may be shocking to you. ... And I'm going to take David [Palmquist] and Kent [Mattox] and Sheryl [Palmquist] this week. They're gonna come with me. You—you—you gonna feel the anointing at Aimee's tomb. It's incredible. And Kathryn's. It's amazing. I've heard of people healed when they visited that tomb. They were totally healed by God's power. You say, 'What a crazy thing.' Brother, there's things we'll never understand. Are you all hearing me?"* [54]

More importantly, **are we hearing what God says about us seeking anything from the dead?**

> *When someone tells you to consult mediums and spiritualists, who whisper and mutter, should not a people inquire of their God? Why consult the dead on behalf of the living?* Isaiah 8:19. [See also Deuteronomy 18:9-14 & Luke 16:19-27.]

Some followers also believe that we should visit heaven on a daily basis, not only to experience special impartations there but also because there are departed saints who are waiting to greet us and give us instructions.

In her book, *Physics of Heaven*, Ellyn Davis writes this about her friend, Judy Franklin, a staff member at Bethel Church in Readding, CA:

> *Judy Franklin has found that people who have a hard time going to heaven by themselves can more easily do it if they are around her so she carries some sort of energy that helps them.*[55]

Rick Joyner, [MorningStarTV.com,Prophetic Perspectives/YouTube/Heaven] teaches that going to heaven is not an option but that we need to go there every day.

> *If you are a true seeker of God, you are going to heaven. I'm not talking about dying and go to heaven. . . We have no choice. We have to go to heaven. We have to start entering into the kingdom more and more every day. It's no longer an option. The world is going to break down into increasing chaos. Those who are going on into Him, they are going to turn and they are going to do these things and those who do not are going to go on into the chaos that the rest of the world is getting into. We have to make the choice and we have to go. It's easy and the best thing we've ever done. The most fun, the most joy and the most peace we have ever had... I was told by Elijah that he and Enoch had been kept alive so that they would not taste death so that they could have a part of the purpose in this last day ministry—the ministry at the end of the age. And I have no problem believing that. Elijah has been appearing to many, and many have been having encounters with him but it's not necromancy because he never died. He's still very much alive. He told me I was supposed to meet Enoch because Enoch had an important message for me.*

**Fire Tunnels**—A common practice at NAR meetings and conferences are "fire tunnels." A fire tunnel is just one way they believe that the "anointing" is received. In a fire tunnel, expectant followers stand in line to receive what they perceive to be a "touch from God." They believe that this is a necessary practice for a believer to be continuously "filled up" with the Holy Spirit so that they will be "equipped" to get to the next level of their spiritual journey.

What exactly are these followers receiving as they proceed through the fire tunnels? Many Christians discern that it is the same spirit as the Hindu *Kundalini* spirit also known as the "serpent power." In Hindu meetings, devotees line up to receive a spiritual experience from a touch by an open hand, (mostly to the forehead) by the guru. After a while, the devotee begins to writhe, shake, jerk, scream, or laugh uncontrollably. The manifestations of the Hindu *Kundalini* and the manifestations demonstrated by NAR believers are almost identical in nature.

**"Slain in the Spirit"**— Another part of the experience that goes along with the fire tunnels that you see at NAR meetings is the whole concept of being "slain in the spirit." It happens when supposedly the power of God comes upon followers—overpowering them physically, so much so that they can no longer stand up—causing them to fall (usually backward) into the arms of another church member called a "catcher." A "catcher" stands behind each one expecting this experience—waiting for the person in case they fall backwards, so he can lay the limp body down to the ground. The same manifestations then occur as the ones in the fire tunnels   People who experience these manifestations believe that it is the Holy Spirit that comes upon them.

> *Let all things be done decently and in order.* I Cor. 14:40

> *That we may lead a tranquil and quiet life in all godliness and dignity.* I Timothy 2:2

Other things one might see at a NAR meeting are glory clouds, gold dust, angel feathers and/or jewels falling from the ceiling. For a more detailed description and video references, see our book, *A Hidden Path—Bethel Redding and Beyond*.

## VI. Strategic Level Spiritual Warfare

Many followers of the New Apostolic Reformation believe in the practice of Strategic Level Spiritual Warfare (SLSW); namely, going after territorial spirits (powerful demons) that allegedly rule over cities, regions, and geographical areas from the second heaven (where they believe that Satan and his demons live). They teach that NAR apostles and believers must take authority over these demons so that the land can be redeemed from all curses and former sins that transpired there. They believe that once SLSW is done, it will enable them to proceed with their goals of taking dominion over that area and, ultimately, the earth. Furthermore, they believe that geographic locations on earth have portals and gateways into which they can access heaven.

Similar practices include—

**Identificational Repentance**—Repenting for sins committed by former generations against people groups such as Jews, Native Americans, and African Americans; for example—sins that have allegedly brought curses on the land.

**Spiritual Mapping**— They believe in the importance of researching the history of certain regions— (1) to identify events that have happened there that may have opened doors to demonic activity, (2) to identify the specific names of the demons that oppress and rule over a specific area and then find the exact places where they loiter. When mapping is done, they go to those places and recite decrees and declarations over the alleged demons, buildings, and the land.

Dr. C. Peter Wagner admitted the following about the fruitlessness of his efforts when his team implemented Strategic Level Spiritual Warfare/Spiritual Mapping in the United States and Japan:

> *Some of the top leadership of the body of Christ have strongly affirmed regional and national transformation as our goal. They have spent huge amounts of time and large sums of money in attempting to push the church forward down this path. But frustration has begun to set in. Even after 10 years, we cannot point to a single city in the United States that has undergone a sociologically verifiable transformation.*[56]
>
> *I was convinced that we had used the weapons of spiritual warfare properly on behalf of that nation (Japan) and that we would literally see the 10 million before 2000. However, it was not to be. Through the 1990's, the rate of church growth in Japan remained unchanged, and the year 2000 saw fewer than 1 million believers in the country— the same number as in 1990, and far short of the 10 million goal . . . This, as you can imagine, was a major disappointment!*[57]

Pastor Bill Randles in his book, *Making War in the Heavenlies, A Different Look*, has contrary views about spiritual warfare over cities and regions:

*The early believers had an attitude towards principalities and powers — not aggressive, militant warfare to pull them down, but confidence that God had set the Church in a position far mightier than any fallen angel. The Christians of the Bible went about preaching the gospel, not in frustration that territorial spirits were cramping their style, but in perfect confidence that God had already won the victory over them.*[58]

*The idea that we are "locked into direct conflict with Satan, toe to toe," is one of the biggest, most unbiblical deceptions today. Satan may be directly attempting to thwart, hinder, tempt, and deceive us, but our resistance to him is based on "submitting to God", not railing at Satan.*[59]

**Yet in the same way these men, also by dreaming, defile the flesh, and reject authority and revile angelic majesties. But Michael the archangel, when he disputed with the devil and argued about the body of Moses, did not dare pronounce against him a railing judgment, but said, "The Lord rebuke you." But these men revile the things which they do not understand; and the things which they know by instinct, like unreasoning animals, by these things they are destroyed.** Jude 8-10.

**Daring, self-willed, they do not tremble when they revile angelic majesties, whereas angels who are greater in might and power do not bring a reviling judgment against them before the Lord.** II Peter 2:10-1

It is interesting to note that John Paul Jackson, deceased, popular author, Christian television personality and a speaker at NAR conferences, cautioned believers about the danger of Strategic Level Spiritual Warfare:

*When we abandon our God-given sphere of authority and engage in second heaven warfare, we stray into a deadly realm where we have no protection or authority, a realm where God never intended his children to be.*[60]

*Although God's people lived under demonic principalities of religion, sexual perversion, and other dark powers; and legions of spirits were spread over the entire Roman Empire, [but] Jesus never addressed them in the second heaven. He only addressed them terrestrially, by ministering to men, women and children, setting them free.*[61]

**Worship**—Worship is a huge venue that the NAR uses to draw unsupecting believers, especially young people, into the movement. Groups such as: Jesus Culture, Hillsong, and Elevation are just a few groups who promote the NAR belief system. Although the songs of these groups portray musical excellence and are pleasing to the ear— they can be hypnotic and seductive when the lyrics are sung over and over again.

A goal of their worship is for believers to create an "atmosphere" that allows them to visit God in the third heaven (where they believe He lives). They teach about an "open heaven"—direct communication between heaven and earth that enables them to experience supernatural impartations there such as: conversations, prophetic words, and instructions from angels and God. They believe that gold dust, jewels, and angel feathers (that sometimes appear in their worship services) are from a heavenly visitation and a precursor to the eventual return of God Himself in full Glory. (see page 19). They also believe they can release "words" back to earth from the third heaven while there.

Another worship goal is to create rhythmic "heavenly", "new" sounds and vibrations. Using worship as a means for spiritual warfare, they believe that they have the ability to release these sounds to break cycles that keep nations in bondage. Bob Jones, deceased, respected NAR prophet reported this about the "new sound":

> *We began having prophecies in 1995 that there is a new sound coming, a new heavenly sound. It's going to come in everything and it's especially going to come in praise. . One time, there was a sound that seemed to be coming out of the ceiling. Everybody heard it. It had an angel power with it. This coming new sound isn't just something that you pick up with your ears, but it's greater than anything you can understand. It can change DNA so we are genetically growing up. Your genetics are the same as His was. Our genetics come out of the Father in our spirit. We are becoming like an instrument being tuned, where our genetics are getting aligned with the Father's genetics, in harmony with Him.*[62]

Chuck Pierce "prophesied" about the "sound" as posted on *The Elijah List* (a NAR respected internet website), "A New Sound of Movement," January 12, 2016:

> *Learn to move by the vibrations of the sound coming up through your feet. This is how I will move my people into place in the days ahead! You will not move by the thoughts of your mind, but by the sounds of heaven vibrating the ground and causing your feet to sense what I am saying so you can move into place for the future.*

NAR believers also teach that before Christ returns, God will transfer control of the world's wealth from the hands of the sinners to the hands of their believers. They are instructed to build and distribute wealth so the church will have the finances to advance their dominion goals. C. Peter Wagner believes this about the importance of wealth:

> *If you want to take a city, you have to buy it. Own businesses, property, and whatever other opportunities you can find to build wealth.*[63]

> *I think that it is time we began agreeing strongly and openly that we cannot expect to be agents in God's hands for massive and sustained reformation unless we control huge amounts of wealth. In all of human history, three things, above all others, have changed society: violence, knowledge and wealth. And the greatest of these is wealth.*[64]

## VII. Conclusion

This booklet is a very brief overview of the agenda and some of the beliefs of those associated with C. Peter Wagner, Chuck Pierce (the present head of the NAR/Global Spheres), and the New Apostolic Reformation. Every Christian and every church, at some point, may have to decide whether or not to simply believe in the Bible as the Word of God or to accept extra-biblical "revelation" from the modern day "apostles" and "prophets" that contradicts or adds to the Word of God. This will be an especially important decision in light of the fact that we are told in the Scriptures that there will be a falling away/apostasy in the end-times. Scriptures tell us to—"guard the treasure that has been entrusted to us", "examine all things carefully", and "test the spirits."

Jesus, Himself, tells us to **"see to it"** that no one deceives us." Warren Smith, in his book, *False Christ Coming, Does Anybody Care?* asks these thought provoking questions:

> *Are Christian leaders leading the church ever closer to the cross—or ever closer to the "Planetary Pentecost"? Why is there almost no call for spiritual discernment within the Church except*

> *to warn believers not to be deceived into doubting their appointed Christian leaders? Why are there so few warnings about a counterfeit New Age/New Spirituality movement that maligns the person of Jesus Christ and threatens the lives of His followers? <u>Why is "spiritual experience" taking precedence over spiritual discernment? Why is "new revelation" in many ministries starting to supersede God's written Word?</u>[65]*

> *Expecting only revival and the return of the true Christ, will people calling themselves Christians be deceived by the one who will come in the name of Christ and pretend to be Him? Caught unawares, will they mistake the counterfeit Christ's "Planetary Pentecost" for the great "move of God" they had been told to expect? Is this all a setup for the great delusion described in the Bible? Is there any good reason not to at least consider this a possibility?[66]*

The early church fathers were adamant and clear about being "sober", "alert", and committed to using discernment when it comes to doctrine. The New Testament has numerous warnings that a great falling away in the end times would come from **within the church** itself.

> ***But false prophets also arose among the people just as there will be false teachers among you who will secretly introduce destructive heresies.*** II Peter 2:1

> ***But the Spirit explicitly says that in later times some will fall away from the faith, paying attention to deceitful spirits and doctrines of demons...*** I Timothy 4:1

> ***For the time will come when they will not endure sound doctrine, but wanting to have their ears tickled. They will accumulate for themselves teachers in accordance to their own desires and will turn away their ears from the truth and will turn aside to myths.*** II Timothy 4:3-5

We have a great concern for many people in the church who are listening to the teachings and "prophetic" words presented in this booklet—and believing them to be truly spoken from God. We know that they are sincere Christians but are unaware and/or deceived.

We have found that some say that they don't want to know—or they think that it's not right to judge. Still others say that they do not believe that these things are really happening. Worse, some turn their cheek and don't see the destruction that unscriptural, false beliefs impose—not only to themselves but also on the whole Christian community.

The purpose of this booklet is not to malign or attack any person or ministry. However, we are told to judge the things that are being spoken and taught by prophets and teachers (I Cor. 14:29). The Apostle Paul preached about love and unity, yet did not hesitate to point out and name those who were false teachers or those who had gone astray. (II Tim. 1:15, II Tim. 2:17-18, II Tim. 4:14)

> *Do not participate in the unfruitful deeds of darkness, but instead even expose them; for it is disgraceful even to speak of the things which are done by them in secret.*
> Ephesians 5:11-12

**OUR PRAYER FOR THE READER.** Father, in Jesus' name, we thank You for all who have read this booklet and have gained understanding to believe and act wisely in the days ahead. May the Holy Spirit give them knowledge so that their foundation in Jesus Christ will be built up—by means of the Word of God and its sound doctrine. Blessings and peace be to them who take the narrow path of truth that leads to life. We ask You, Lord, for discernment especially in the days ahead, so that we can stand firm and hold to the sound doctrine which we were taught. In Jesus' Name. Amen.

> *An appalling and horrible thing*
> *Has happened in the land: The prophets prophesy falsely,*
> *And the priests run on their own authority:*
> *And my people love it so—*
> *But what will you do at the end of it? Jer. 5:30-31*

## Endnotes

1. Cindy Jacobs, *The Reformation Manifesto,* Bethany Publishers, Bloomington, MN, 2008, p. 18-19
2. Ibid,, p. 10
3. Ibid., p. 10
4. C. Peter Wagner, *Dominion*, Chosen Books, Grand Rapids, MI, 2008, p. 24

5. C. Peter Wagner, *Wrestling with Alligators, Prophets and Theologians*, Regal, Ventura, CA, p. 213
6. C. Pete Wagner, *Churchquake*, Regal, Ventura, CA, 1999, p. 49
7. Op cit, Wrestling with Alligators, p. 215
8. Warren B. Smith, *False Christ Coming, Does Anybody Care?*, Mountain Stream Press, Magalia, CA, 2011, p. 53
9. Ibid., p. 52
10. Ibid., p. 76
11. Ibid., p. 75
12. Ibid., p. 91
13. Ibid., p.77
14. Ibid., p. 124
15. Cumby, Constance, *The Hidden Dangers of the Rainbow*, Huntington House, Inc., 1983, p. 115
16. Ray Yungen, *A Time of Departing*, Lighthouse Trails Publishing, Silverton, OR, p. 120
17. C. Peter Wagner, *On Earth As It Is In Heaven*, Regal, Ventura, CA, 2012, p. 48
18. Op cit., C. Peter Wagner, *Wrestling with Alligators*, p. 256
19. Op cit., C. Peter Wagner, *On Earth as it is in Heaven*, p. 74 (quoting Steve Thompson, *The Morning Star Journal*, Summer, 2006, p. 22
20. Johnny Enlow, *The Seven Mountain Prophesy*, Creation House, Lake Mary, FL, 2008, p. 23-24
21. Bill Johnson, When Heaven Invades Earth, Destiny Image Publishers, Inc., Shippensburg, PA, 2003, p. 29
22. https://www.youtube.com/watch?v=EhG1x4fOtBw
23. Op cit., Bill Johnson, *When Heaven Invades Earth*, p. 76
24. Ibid., p. 24
25. Op cit., Dr. Bill Hamon, *Apostles, Prophets*, p. 361
26. Keith Gibson, *Wandering Stars*, Solid Ground Christian Books, Vestavia, AL, 2011, p. 207 (quoting Francis Frangipane) *In the Presence of God*, New Wine Press, Sussex, England, 1994, p. 154
27. Ibid., p. 206
28. Op cit., Dr. Bill Hamon, *Apostles, Prophets*, p. 361
29. Rick Joyner, *The Harvest*, 1989-1990 revised booklet, p. 121
30. Op cit., Dr. Bill Hamon, *The Eternal Church*, p. 323
31. Op cit., C. Peter Wagner, *Dominion*, p. 61
32. Ibid., p. 61
33. Op cit., Dr. Bill Hamon, *The Eternal Church*, p. 359-360
34. C. Peter Wagner, *Changing Church*, Regal, Ventura, CA, 2004, p. 35
35. Ibid., p. 36
36. Op cit., C. Peter Wagner, Churchquake, p. 112 (quoting John Kelly)
37. Dr. Bill Hamon, *Apostles, Prophets and the Coming Move of God*, Destiny Image Publishers, Shippensburg, PA, 1997, p. 153
38. Ibid., p. 223

39. Dr. Bill Hamon, *The Eternal Church*, Destiny Image Publishers, Shippensburg, PA, 1981, p. 298
40. Ibid., p. 316
41. C. Peter Wagner, *Church in the Workplace*, Regal, Ventura, CA 2006, p. 7-8
42. Ask Mike Bickle, Are Dreams, Visions, and Visitations Higher Than the Work of God?, You Tube
43. Dr. Bill Hamon, Prophets and Personal Prophesy, Christian International, Santa Rosa Beach, FL, 1987, p. 19
44. Johnny Enlow, *The Elijah List*, Rosh Hashanah, 2014: Year of Secrets Revealed, September, 2014
45. Op cit., *On Earth As It Is In Heaven*, p. 149
46. C. Peter Wagner, Confronting the Powers, Regal, Ventura, CA 1996, p. 147-148
47. Bill Johnson, Dreaming with God, Destiny Image Publishers, Shippensburg, PA 2006, p. 86
48. Judy Franklin and Ellyn Davis, The Physics of Heaven, (written by Jonathan Welton), Double Portion Publishing, Crossville, TN, 2012, p. 49
49. Ibid., p. 103 (written by Larry Randolph)
50. Op cit., Warren B. Smith, False Christ Coming, p. 12
51. Op cit., Judy Franklin and Ellyn Davis, The Physics of Heaven, p. 31 (written by Bill Johnson)
52. Ibid., p 37
53. Op cit., Dr. Bill Hamon, *Apostles, Prophets*, p. 235
54. Benny Hinn sermon, Double Portion Anointing, Part 3, Orlando Christian Center, 4/4/91, Sermon series TV#309 obtained from Personal Freedom Outreach
55. Op cit., Judy Franklin and Ellyn Davis, *Physics of Heaven*, p. 53
56. Op cit., C. Peter Wagner, *Changing Church*, p. 96
57. Op cit., C. Peter Wagner, Wrestling with Aligators, *p. 236-238*
58. Pastor Bill Randles, *Making War in the Heavenlies*, A Different Look, St. Matthew Publication, Great Britain, 1994, p. 28
59. Ibid., p. 85
60. John Paul Jackson, *Needless Casualties of War*, Streams Publishing, North Sutton, NJ, 1999, p. 101
61. Ibid., p. 94
62. Op cit., Judy Franklin and Ellyn Davis, *The Physics of Heaven*, p. 25-26 (written by Bob Jones)
63. Op cit., C. Peter Wagner, *On Earth As It Is In Heaven*, p. 182
64. Op cit., C. Peter Wagner, *Wrestling with Alligators*, p. 265
65. Op cit., Warren B. Smith, *False Christ Coming, p. 119*
66. Ibid., p. 119

# Volume II
# Narrow is the Way—
# Have You Really Found It?

A Sound Word Ministry Publication

## *Narrow is the Way—Have You Really Found It?*
© May, 2020

ISBN # 978-1-64871-559-4

1st edition – June, 2016
2nd edition – July, 2016
3rd edition - May, 2020

## Compiled by M. Barbara Hansell
Cover layout and design by Oscar J. Whatmore

**Authors:** David Choiniere   Angie Deets   M. Barbara Hansell
J. F. Keenan   Maria Chadim Kirkpatrick   Joy McCloud   Tricia Pell
Jason Snider   Oscar J. Whatmore

**Much appreciation to Robert H.** for the many hours spent editing, layout, and support. Thanks to Mary Lou Graeber for proofreading.

Front Cover photo by: Shutterstock – Mikael Damkier (Used by permission)
Back Cover photo by: Shutterstock – Sergey Nivens   (Used by permission)

**Copyright Disclaimer—**Under Section 107 of the Copyright Act of 1976, allowance is made for fair use for purposes such as criticism, comment, news reporting, teaching, scholarship, and research.

**Authors of this booklet can be reached at—**
USA:      soundwordministry1@gmail.com
Europe:   oscarwhatmore@gmail.com

*Now to Him who is able to keep you from stumbling, and to make you stand in the presence of His glory blameless with great joy, to the only God our Savior, through Jesus Christ our Lord, be glory, majesty, dominion, and authority, before all time and now and forever. Amen.* Jude 24

## DEDICATION

This book is dedicated to Bob Brunette – for his vision of establishing an online network of thousands of like-minded believers, seeking truth worldwide.

## TABLE OF CONTENTS

### VOLUME 2 – Narrow is the Way – Have You Really Found It?

Oscar Whatmore – England ---------------------------------------------------------39

Maria Chadim Kirkpatrick – USA----------------------------------------------------45

J. F. Keenan – USA ------------------------------------------------------------------50

Angie Deets – USA ------------------------------------------------------------------56

David Choiniere – Guatemala-------------------------------------------------------60

M. Barbara Hansell – USA ----------------------------------------------------------64

Tricia Pell – USA ---------------------------------------------------------------------70

Joy McCloud – USA -----------------------------------------------------------------75

Jason Snider – USA------------------------------------------------------------------81

# AUTHORS' NOTE

### WHO WE ARE AND WHY WE WROTE THIS BOOK

We are nine born-again believers from three countries, who share the following things in common—(1) We all love the Lord Jesus Christ, (2) We all have been exposed to the NEW APOSTOLIC REFORMATION (NAR), (3) We all, individually and collectively, discern that although the NAR is very popular in the body of Christ today and growing huge in magnitude; it is a false move of God because it does not adhere to: the teachings of Jesus Christ, the Holy Scriptures, or the apostles' practices contained in the gospels or the Book of Acts, and (4) we all have great concerns for the thousands of sincere believers who are either unaware or deceived who remain in NAR churches around the world.

This book contains real testimonies by actual believers. The purpose of this book is not to malign or attack any person or ministry. It was not written out of any kind of bitterness or contempt for church leaders or any particular ministry—but out of the concerns we share about deception we see in the church today, along with our commitment to uphold the integrity of the Bible and sound doctrine.

> *Do not participate in the unfruitful deeds of darkness, but instead even expose them; for it is disgraceful even to speak of the things which are done by them in secret.* Ephesians 5:11-12

# OSCAR J. WHATMORE—England

In 2003, after coming from a fairly conservative church background, my then wife and children and I joined a Vineyard church in England. From the first service, I was impressed with the pastor's teaching. He was clearly intelligent (an Oxford graduate), and was very good at expounding scripture and exhorting his listeners to apply the Word to their lives. It was clear that he spent a lot of time studying and held the faithful teaching of the Bible as a very high value. The sense of community and family was also very strong.

It wasn't long before we were volunteering to serve—turning up early and leaving late to set up and pack down most Sundays, helping with the kids' activities, making tea and coffee, and I played the drums in the worship band. Within about 18 months, we were leading a house group and, soon after that, I was preaching in the main services on a regular basis.

At this stage, the focus of the church was very much on worship as a lifestyle, which necessarily involved biblical discipleship, and the preaching of the Gospel of Jesus Christ. It was obviously more nuanced than that, but on the whole, it was a good, biblical church (at least that was my impression of it), and a church that I was excited to be a part of. It's hard to pinpoint when and how the change came. However, by the end of 2006, something had fundamentally changed, though it would take several years to render the church unrecognisable from the one I'd joined.

In 2007, I attended a conference with a large group from church. One of the key speakers was Bill Johnson, senior leader of Bethel Church, Redding, California. This was the first time I'd heard him speak.

My main memory was that, as he spoke, I was "scratching my head" trying to figure out how he'd arrived at his interpretation of a particular scripture he was quoting from. I actually thought to myself that he must be making it up as he goes along. But then I looked around at my friends and trusted pastors, who were all nodding and furiously taking notes, and they just seemed to be "getting it." The thought occurred to me that maybe it was just me—maybe it was my own lack of understanding or faith that was preventing me from accepting what was being taught. In a moment that I rue to this day, I chose to ignore the warning bells ringing in my head, abandon my God-given intelligence, and follow the crowd. **THIS MARKED THE BEGINNING OF A LANDSLIDE THAT WOULD ULTIMATELY WRECK MY FAITH, MY FAMILY, MOST OF MY FRIENDSHIPS, AND MY MENTAL HEALTH**.

Between 2007 and 2014, my former church underwent extensive changes as it came increasingly under the influence of Bethel Church and other New Apostolic Reformation teachings. Here are some examples of the changes that were made—

**OUT WENT SUPPLICATION**—Making requests to God in prayer, e.g. "give us this day our daily bread." **IN CAME DECLARATION,** the use of presumptuous language, e.g. "I declare/pull down/release financial breakthrough." Such declaration effectively leaves God out of the conversation and takes the focus away from Him and onto our "faith." Not only is this **NOT** prayer, we were taught that making such declarations was, in fact, prophetic—yet these "prophecies" were not subject to the scrutiny and accountability required in Scripture.

*[margin note: Sarah declared that certain stats would NOT apply to her students]*

**OUT WENT EVANGELISM/MAKING DISCIPLES**—Communicating the biblical gospel to non-believers and teaching and training converts in the Christian life. **IN CAME MOTIVATIONALISM**—One of the last services I attended was a Christmas carol service. I estimated that at least half of those who attended had been invited by church members. The pastor stood before the crowd and told them that the message of Christmas was that God wants to say "yes" to their dreams. **IN CAME MYSTICISM/OCCULT PRACTICES**—one example of this was when a group of us did an "outreach" in a pub. We set ourselves up at a table and left a notice on the bar, inviting people to receive a "spiritual reading." Our brief was to give people "prophetic words" but were instructed not to talk about Jesus or the ACTUAL gospel message of sin, repentance & salvation. **IN CAME CULTURE**—Influencing the culture (as per the NAR Seven Mountains Mandate) somehow came to replace disciple-making, as if persuading people to accept an alternative set of cultural norms and values would ever produce a genuine disciple of Jesus!

**OUT WENT EXEGESIS**—Reading scripture in context; objectively drawing out the intended meaning from the text, and teaching it to others. **IN CAME EISEGESIS**—Taking scripture out of context, ignoring the intended meaning, applying subjective meanings and teaching these things to others.

*[margin note: Sarah allowed a student to completely misinterpret Romans 9:20 and speak in front of all Higher Ground]*

40

**OUT WENT QUOTING THE BIBLE**—In general conversation and when discussing matters of doctrine. **IN CAME QUOTING NAR LEADERS**—It became commonplace to have discussions concluded definitively with "Well, Bill Johnson says. . ."

**OUT WENT TESTING/USING DISCERNMENT**—Scripture commands us over and over to not accept every wave of teaching or word of prophecy, but to test all things against God's revealed Word. **IN CAME "TOUCH NOT THE LORD'S ANOINTED"**—Anything less than wholesale acceptance of the teachings and "prophetic" utterings of the NAR leaders carried the strong implication that your faith was lacking, that you had a critical, rebellious or religious spirit, that you were divisive, or even that you were against God Himself! **IN CAME FALSE PROPHECY**—This became absolutely rampant! "Prophecies" given out like they're two a penny; many of which were so lacking in substance or specifics as to be useless and untestable, and others that were clearly just telling recipients what they wanted to hear. Those giving the "prophecies" were not subject to the accountability required in scripture, even when the "prophecies" were demonstrably false.

**OUT WENT REALITY**—Living in the real world, acknowledging that good and bad things happen to people regardless of how relatively "good" they may be, because there is sin and evil in the world. **IN CAME UNREALITY**—Driven by the lie of "positive thinking" and the false belief that God is somehow more or less able to bless us depending on what we believe about Him, ourselves, or—the reality of a given situation. **IN CAME TRIPS TO HEAVEN**—Yes, we even had practical teaching on how to visit heaven from the comfort of our chair! In reality, this was no more than a phony visualisation exercise. But because it was believed/assumed to be genuine, you could give your own account of what you saw, heard and experienced on your "trip," and no one could question your claims—no matter how bizarre or out of line with scripture they were. **IN CAME DELUSION**—I say without humour that continued exposure to and indulgence in "positivity" (which is in fact—reality/denial) can cause serious and long-lasting damage to your mental health. If reality denial, playing down or dismissing "negativity" (unpalatable realities) and over emphasising "positives" becomes normal for you—then you've become delusional!

I've really only "scratched the surface," but you can hopefully see that what the church became was not the church I thought I'd joined years earlier.

I struggled with these things over several years; but I somehow always let myself be convinced that it was my own lack of faith, or that I just "hadn't gotten there yet." This all got so deeply under my skin that I concluded that I must've been going through a faith crisis. In a sense, I was! But I have since realised that it wasn't as simple as no longer believing in Christianity. It was more the case that the false Christianity I'd bought from the NAR (via my church) had crowded out and shouted louder than the truth. I also interpreted my struggle with believing the NAR lies (even though I, myself, also preached them—God have mercy!) to mean that I no longer believed at all. Whatever the case, I was about ready to renounce Christianity and walk away altogether! **THIS IS THE RISK FOR ALL WHO BUY INTO THE NEW APOSTOLIC REFORMATION—DELUSION OR DISILLUSIONMENT (OR BOTH) AND LOSS OF FAITH IN TRUE, BIBLICAL CHRISTIANITY.**

The less biblical the teaching and practices, the more controlling and dogmatic the environment and leadership style became. I was once told that—"God is doing a new thing," that Christians would no longer gather around doctrines or denominations, but around "fathers" (namely Bill Johnson, John Arnott, and other NAR leaders), that the New Apostolic Reformation was God's model for the church in the 21$^{st}$ century, and I had to choose whether I was going to get onboard or miss out on what God was doing on the earth. In other words, I was either for the NAR or against God! I took these words very seriously, as I had a lot of respect for the guy who said them. Furthermore, because I had nearly enough abandoned discernment, it became a threat in my mind—that **IF I DIDN'T ACCEPT ALL OF THE TEACHING OF THE NAR ELITE** (including the likes of Todd Bentley and Heidi Baker), **I WOULD BE PLACING MYSELF IN OPPOSITION TO GOD HIMSELF.**

Another subtle and cruel device of control that was frequently employed was talking about destiny, hopes, and dreams; and then actively discouraging people from pursuing their own dreams. An oft quoted scripture was Matthew 10:41. *He who receives a prophet in the name of a prophet shall receive a prophet's reward.* This was interpreted to mean that in honouring the pastor, for example, by essentially laying down your dreams to serve his, God would reward you (eventually) by bringing your dreams about. What this did was to effectively make the fulfilment of my own dreams and destiny dependent on how well and how faithfully I served the church—when all the while, years were passing by, and many opportunities with them.

Lots of people left the church over this period including several prominent leaders. In the cases of those who'd previously been well respected, long serving leaders—it was always controversial. In each instance, the pastors would inform the remaining leaders that—the person(s) had a "heart issue," were unwilling to "serve the vision" (of the pastors), that "the real them had come out," that they had a "rebellious and/or critical spirit," or, as in the case of a lady who'd tirelessly served the church as a children's worker and worship leader for nearly a decade—"had a Jezebel spirit." I don't recall that the pastors ever accepted responsibility for the breakdown in a relationship; nor that they ever gave consideration to the possibility that the common threads running through the disagreements that led to each breakdown could be highlighting flaws in their leadership. The way these fallouts were handled by the pastors became a subtle (or perhaps not so subtle!) instrument of control over those who remained. Long before I finally left the church (in 2014), I'd had thoughts of leaving. I had even "decided" to leave several times, but realised that history showed there was no easy way out, that no one I knew of in leadership (as I was) had ever simply left. It had always been a very public breakdown, and they had always been discussed disparagingly and virtually excommunicated afterwards. I didn't want to join that number—and so I stayed!

Of all the NAR centres, Bethel was especially (though by no means exclusively) promoted, and its leaders were revered in the church. Over a number of years, we hosted several people from Bethel including Bethel School of Supernatural Ministry students and various ministry leaders—including the guy who taught us how to visit heaven. It was always impressed upon us what a great honour it was for us to have these people visiting all the way from the States and investing in our church. The uncritical, wholesale embrace of all things Bethel was such that it seemed that if it were from Bethel, it **had** to be right and good!

That was until one of them left his wife in California to be with my wife in England! Interestingly enough, once their affair had become public, the pastor played down and even denied the fact that he was from

Bethel. Yes, he had attended Bethel, but (according to the pastor) he didn't represent them nor was he promoted by them. Strange then that you could (at the time) buy his DVD's from Bethel's online shop. In any case, this affair spelt the end of both the marriages involved and marked the beginning of the end of my time at that church.

Over the subsequent months, I found it harder and harder to attend, partly because of how publicly my marriage had crashed and burned. It was also because I'd taken some time to reflect and found that I could no longer deny the major struggles I'd been having with just about everything to do with that church—not least the numerous and manifestly false prophecies I'd received prior to my marriage break-up. The church had a number of people who allegedly "moved in the prophetic." Over the months that my ex-wife was engaged in her secret affair, these "prophets" had prophesied, indeed had **declared**, that our marriage was entering a season of great blessing and joy, etc. These "prophecies" continued right up until the Sunday before the affair came out and we separated—never to return. According to Deuteronomy 18:20-22, that makes them false prophets, which was a major problem for me, since it represented a significant proportion of the leadership, including the pastors Not only that, but the Sunday services continued to look less and less like a church and more and more like a circus, and it was becoming unbearable!

After a few months, I was only attending occasionally, and I think the distance this created helped me to see with greater clarity just how far from biblical Christianity the church had strayed. The second to last service I attended was the Christmas service I mentioned earlier. As I sat there listening to the non-gospel message, I became aware that I was literally shaking my head in dismay, but I didn't care who saw! So I just carried on shaking my head in disgust at the squandered opportunity for the pastor to tell the real message of Christmas. I went once more after that, and it was just more of the same; so I said to myself as I left that day that I would never go back. Walking away for the last time, I felt like I'd escaped from something. It was both exhilarating and terrifying!

However, that wasn't the end of the story. Even though I was no longer a member of the church, and despite the fact that most had chosen not to call me during the worst time of my life, it would occasionally get back to me that I was being discussed and my "choices" disapproved of.

Additionally, because I'd begun to speak out against the NAR on social media, I found myself being rebuked to my face and via email. It was more than I could take at the time, as I was still reeling from the events of the previous couple of years. I felt very abandoned and yet somehow still subject to the church. The church had taken such a huge toll on me in every regard, and had left me with nothing except an all but destroyed faith. I began to fear walking through town, in case I saw someone from church who'd want to quiz me on my "choices." This became so severe that it led me to constantly looking over my shoulder and even having panic attacks. I finally reached a point where the only thing I could do to make life tolerable was to move to a new town!

Since then, my perspective has become clearer and clearer and I can see just how deceived and controlled I'd become. I've learned that behind the lies and deceit, there was a spiritual dynamic at work which aided my acceptance of them. <u>I've learned the hard way that knowing the truth is my responsibility—that I can't sit back and blindly trust the person behind the microphone to tell me the truth, or to even care about the truth.</u>

**A FINAL THOUGHT**: I was lied to! A poor counterfeit was sold to me by a cartel of con artists and charlatans!—**BUT**—it was my choice to get in line and exchange gold for garbage!

## MARIA CHADIM KIRKPATRICK—United States

Nothing made sense anymore, and I didn't know what to believe. I spent months researching—combing the Word of God as well as the internet for anything related to what I had been subjected to. In doing so, the truth finally came to light. I was deeply involved with a religious system called the New Apostolic Reformation (NAR). Our church was under the "covering" of a non-denominational ministry, which hails from Santa Rosa Beach, Florida. As I began to dig deep into the roots of the organization and its founder, the truth started to reveal itself. It was a revelation that forever changed me, a revelation which turned my world upside-down. This revelation set me free from false doctrine and helped place me on the narrow path spoken about in Matthew 7: 13-16(a).

I was traumatized, isolated, scared, troubled, confused, and betrayed! My trust was gone, and my faith was shaken to the core! I had just left the community which was my church—a fellowship in which I prayed, confided, trusted, and loved. I was left with many questions: 'What was my purpose?' 'What was my calling?' My church gave me a false sense of purpose. I now wanted to know what God's purpose was for my life.

I never felt right about being in that congregation; something was always "off," but I couldn't put my finger on it: it was the New Apostolic Reformation—NAR! But the NAR was not something which was spoken about in my fellowship or by my pastors. In fact, I didn't hear that term until my research began. The roots ran deep. The movement had other titles throughout the years. It was nothing "new." To say that I was shocked to learn the truth was an understatement!

The church was advertised as being Word-based and Spirit-filled, yet the Scriptures were taken out of context regularly. As weeks turned into months, and months turned into years, that feeling of something being "off" continued to get stronger. I began to check the pastor's sermons with the Word of God, and they didn't match. I finally realized that **ANOTHER GOSPEL WAS BEING PREACHED—ANOTHER JESUS WAS WORSHIPPED.** I was stunned!

Initially, unbeknownst to us, we were deeply involved in the pastors' "inner circle"—the closest of the close. We were given the title of "leaders" without ever being asked. With that title came new responsibilities which would lead us down a dark path of spiritual, emotional, and financial abuse. We blindly followed the lead of the pastors without ever, at the onset, questioning their authority or motives. We were promised extra blessings, financial breakthrough, relational healing, and more—if we did as we were told. We believed in the things that were promised and the "prophecies" which we received. Needless to say, we found ourselves "bewitched" like the Galatians were.

During our tenure as top, inner circle leaders, my husband and I spent over a year and a half of our lives, day in and day out with the pastors. They asked for our help with the renovation of their new home for which they did not pay one dime! The initial agreement was to assist them for three weeks at no cost to them, but they manipulated us through prophetic "words" and "favor"—to extend that help way beyond anything that we would have agreed to on our own both time-wise and financially. Looking back though, this allowed us to be privy to personal information (pertaining to the pastors, their families and congregants), as well as privy to their attitudes, values, and secrets. Once again, their words and behavior did not match what was being spoken, prophesied, taught, and commanded from others in the congregation. They constantly cried, "poor" all the while taking trips to places like Mexico, Florida, the Coastal Carolinas and Pennsylvania for special conferences put on by the main ministry in Florida. We did not realize this at first, because we were slowly and methodologically being taken advantage of through domination, manipulation, and intimidation. By the time we put it all together we figured out that **WE WERE BEING CONTROLLED UNAWARE!**

The control began slowly at first. We were questioned by the pastors if we missed a service or meeting. They wanted to know why we weren't there and what was more important than attendance. Later, we were asked if we knew why others weren't there and if the others had attended another fellowship. The pastor placed me as a watchman in the church. I had to report everything that I saw and heard, comments which were contrary to him, his family, or his teachings. My husband was the head of security and was asked to watch for "suspicious visitors." Eventually, the contact increased from one phone call or text per week to ten-plus calls or texts daily. **CHURCH BECAME OUR LIFE!** The pastor(s) had every minute of our days planned. Our home life became neglected as we ran to and from the church and all of its various classes and activities. I was overwhelmed and knew I couldn't keep up the pace. We did this for over three years. Enough was enough! When I brought it to the attention of the pastor, I was told that "I had a spirit of rebellion and that I needed deliverance followed by repentance." That was the modus operandi every time an issue was brought before the pastor(s) with which they didn't agree.

To make matters worse, the church was run by a board, which consisted of the pastor's family (his wife, his two daughters and their husbands, his son and his son's wife and himself). The board positions were reserved for two of his children and their spouses—even though they lived out of state and rarely attended a service. There was no opportunity for members of the congregation to serve on the board. Also there was no accountability within the ranks of the board. You couldn't question them or their decisions without being severely reprimanded by the pastors. There was no one else to go to for help. If you dared to cross them, you would be pointed out and mocked in front of the congregation. They were harder on those closest to them and I was publicly called out and mocked on many occasions. **THEY CONTROLLED THE CONGREGATION WITH FEAR, AND I WAS AFRAID**!

Another issue that quickly became apparent was that our fellowship spoke in its own language—Christianese! Certain words and phrases that I had never heard before were regularly used by the pastors and congregants: Words such as—*decree, declare, paradigm-shift, anointing, region, activate,* and *Pharisee,* were spoken in almost every sentence. Phrases such as—*slain in the spirit, touch not God's anointed, accessing the gates (of Heaven), for such a time as this, we need to move past the cross, God is doing a new thing, Strategic Level Spiritual Warfare, going to another level, going deeper, glory cloud, dreams and visions, prophetic word,* and *changing the atmosphere* were phrases that dominated conversations, teachings, and sermons. We were taught that we were to be "reproducers of reproducers"—and that the apostles would transfer the apostolic anointing, and that the prophets would transfer the prophetic anointing. We were taught that we were an end-times army and that the pastor was our general.

According to the pastor, we were constantly "under attack" by the enemy. Those attacks included congregants who decided to leave the church. We were also taught that, if our prayers weren't being answered, if sicknesses were not being healed, or if we had financial problems—then **WE DIDN'T HAVE ENOUGH FAITH!** The pastors were arrogant, demanding, pompous, and (in their own minds)—infallible. The pastor once stated that "I can't be deceived—I'm above that—My wife and I have to be!" But contrary to the statements that he proclaimed about himself and his wife, he would preach that anyone who thought that they could not be deceived, already was deceived.

We were told that no other church like ours existed in our region! We were taught to believe that we were closer to God than Christians who strictly relied on the Word of God. We were chasing experiences, signs, wonders, and miracles. I believed that I was doing the will of the Lord—until I decided to compare what I was doing with scriptures such as Matthew 7: 15-23. Other Bible passages began hitting me like bolts of lightning. For the first time, my eyes began to open, and I started to see that **I WAS INVOLVED WITH OTHER DOCTRINES—DOCTRINES OF DEVILS!**

The focus of the genuine church is on the entire Word of God—the Gospel of Jesus Christ, and the Holy Spirit. But, at my former church, we were solely focused on the moves of the Holy Spirit. We would beg Him to come into our presence through music and prayer. We would plead for His fire to fall and consume us, for the glory cloud to overtake us, and for us to be translated into the throne room of God. We would be told to pray harder, longer and with more faith, making decrees and declarations, soaking in His presence and fasting. We were required to read all of the books written by our church founder as opposed to being encouraged to read the Bible.

As covenant members, we couldn't attend another church or another church function without the pastor's expressed permission. He would scan Facebook pages, Instagrams and Twitter, looking for photos or statements of congregants who attended other events or conferences. If you were caught, you were accused of being "out of order" and "in rebellion" to him and to God. Our pastors had one foot in the Law and one foot in grace. We slowly evolved into a congregation where works and legalism became commonplace. If you do "this," you will reap "that." For example, if we were at church fifteen minutes early on Sunday, attended Thursday night workshops, extra services, leadership meetings, fellowship dinners—it was proclaimed that we would receive "extra blessings," a "double anointing," a "double portion," "financial favor," and "miraculous physical healing." We were told that those who did not do all of the above things would miss out on the blessing and possibly be under a "curse!" Guilt was placed on those who were not in attendance from the pulpit on Sunday mornings.

A hint of the Hebrew Roots Movement permeated our fellowship as well. We would pray while wearing a tallit; men wore Kippahs (skull caps) at certain services; and we were compelled to celebrate certain Jewish feasts—in order to receive a special blessing. Also we were verbally condemned if we didn't tithe 10% of our income to the church.

People were "slain in the spirit" every time we met—along with screaming, moaning, twitching, jerking, shaking and rocking back and forth. Bodies strewn about the floor was a common sight. (I have since come to learn through my research that these very signs are also part of the Hindu religion and the Kundalini Spirit.) Those who did not "fall-out" were questioned and verbally chastised for not allowing the Holy Spirit to "move" in their lives. Congregants were addicted to receiving "prophetic words" and would line up after services to have the pastors pray and "prophesy" over them. (This reminded me of going to a psychic for a reading.)

We were required to sign a covenant with the church in order to become members. When we sent in our letter of resignation, the pastor threatened not to "release us." He told us that if we were not "released," we would be under a curse, because we "touched God's anointed" (meaning him). We told him that we did not need a "release." Such a thing is found nowhere in the Bible. We told him that God gave us a free will, and we were exercising that by leaving!

There is not enough space in this booklet to tell about all of what we were subjected to as a result of our initial lack of knowledge of God's Word. I have left out specific incidents of abuse which were perpetrated upon my family through and by the actions and words of the co-pastors, who sold themselves as apostles and prophets of God. Instead, I focused on the overall, unbiblical issues which permeate the cultic nature of this false movement.

At the time of this writing, it has been a little over a year and a half (we permanently left on August 28, 2015) since we left our former church. Healing has begun to take place with the help of others, like me, who have also left the movement known as the New Apostolic Reformation. When I left, there was little to be found regarding actual testimonies of those who came out. I believe that the Lord allowed me to experience this false movement in order that I may reach others with my testimony—others who want to leave. For a long time after I left, I was confused as to what my purpose in life was. Now I thank the Lord each and every day for allowing me to experience something which I can use to help others who are finding themselves in the same, seemingly hopeless position that I once occupied. **YOU ARE NOT ALONE!**

## J. F. KEENAN—United States

I did not have much of a background in Christianity growing up. I accepted Jesus into my heart when I was 16 years old and was born again. I attended a strong Bible-believing, Bible-teaching Assemblies of God church that taught about the gifts of the Spirit. For the next four years, I developed a love for the Word of God, and I was consumed and very well versed in the New Testament.

I joined the military and was there for the next three years. I had a strong group of Christian friends, and we remained faithful to the teachings of the Scriptures. I continued to study the New Testament and taught an adult Bible class. When I eventually left the military, I ended up working at an Assemblies of God church in Texas. I was an associate pastor there working with the young adults and youth.

By late 1995, I became a licensed minister in the Assemblies of God. I was in contact with over 120 ministers in my district and I seemed to gravitate towards the older, very wise, seasoned men of God that had stood the test of time. I had a habit of asking them many hard, theological questions because I was always a lover of truth; and, most importantly, I desired to walk in His truth. I left Texas in order to attend Valley Forge Christian College and started taking Bible classes there. As usual, I always gravitated towards the more serious professors that had a deep love for the Word of God. In addition, I made strong, good relationships from the president on down to interim professors. I relinquished my licensure with the Assemblies of God after realizing that being a pastor was not my calling, but I remained faithful to studying God's Word and living for the Lord. I continued to teach adult classes in various churches during that time.

Over the next 13 years, my family and I spent time in various kinds of independent, Assemblies of God, and Bible-believing charismatic/Pentecostal churches. Consequently, some friends told me about a small, evangelical church where the pastor was sincerely seeking a deeper relationship with God. I bonded with him immediately, and a close relationship developed. He often invited me to go to various church meetings and conferences, and I was given the opportunity to participate with the leaders of these meetings. The pitch was that we needed "apostolic" covering in order to walk with the Lord in greater love, greater power, and greater truth. Under those circumstances, what Christian would not want to be there on account of their love for Him?

Even though not officially a leader in the church, I was invited by my pastor to the closed, insider meetings to participate in the inner workings of the "apostolic" leadership and its development. There was an allure that we would receive more privileged information from the "apostles" and "prophets" if we joined, and I became part of their system. They said that they "had something that nobody else had" and that "we had much more to experience." They told us that if we joined them, we would be privy to the "revelation knowledge" God was revealing to them for the church. I was offered a membership so that I could be a part of the growing movement of the "mighty hand of God," and I was invited to join their network of "apostles" and prophets' guidance teams—if I paid the initiation fees and yearly dues.

They didn't tell me about the hidden, dominionist agenda behind this movement or even its name. I found out later on my own—it was The New Apostolic Reformation!

As we went to these large open and sometimes "by invitation only" meetings, I went with what I thought was a strong, biblical understanding and with a guarded mind and a cautious heart. In our private conversations with my pastor, I made it very plain to him that I had seen, from times past—multitudes of things that were said to be of the Spirit of God, yet I was highly unimpressed; and I always looked for the fruit that manifested. I explained to him that I was hard to impress with any type of man-made hype. In fact, even if they raised somebody from the dead, I would want to see the clinical documentation that the one raised—actually was clinically dead. Most importantly, I wanted to discern what spirit was behind it all.

In spite of that, I eagerly attended these meetings and conferences. I saw people who said that they were "apostles" and "prophets" who claimed to hand out "words from the Lord" to hundreds and hundreds of people. The interesting thing was that many of these "prophesies" contained an element of truth to them. I received at least ten "prophesies" that were generally correct. Because of the accuracy, I assumed that the "prophets" must be hearing from God; and hence, this became another hook for me to continue to be a part. However, I realize now that there were people in the Bible such as Jannes and Jambres, Pharoah's magicians, who also moved in supernatural power to the point of having the ability to copy six of the ten plagues against Egypt. I realize now more than ever that the supernatural signs alone are not a means of discernment—rather the Word of God is!

I saw that the teachings of the NAR "apostles" were 95% centered around the works of other men and not the Scriptures. It all sounded really good, at first; and the whole situation seemed as though it blended together like a good suit. In all of this, I had a prick in my soul that I could not shake; however, I wanted to ignore it so that I could believe in my heart that this movement was truly a work of God. I was brought into places where all the people seemed to be experiencing a joyful, ecstatic experience with the Lord. I felt like I was being drawn in. The people surrounding me were good people who loved the Lord—people that were "drinking" as if they had just come from the desert and had run out of water. I didn't want to be contrary and not be part of what God **might** be doing. They asked me, "Don't you want to be part of a "new move of God" and receive more love, more power, and more truth?" They implied that I needed to be there, or else I would miss something God was doing. That prick of the Holy Spirit in the back of my soul which told me that something wasn't right, wouldn't shut off. Consequently, I was confused and conflicted!

*[handwritten note: Sounds like Tiffany a little bit]*

All the teachings from these "apostles" and "leaders" made a tremendous amount of sense—until I compared their teachings to the Bible. They took their bizarre doctrines and wrapped the Scriptures around it. As I studied the Word of God in comparison to what was being taught, such as—in order to receive the title of an "apostle," all you needed to do is to have enough of the correct people from the organization ("apostles" claiming to be carriers of this new "anointing") proclaim that you are one. I also witnessed crazy, uncontrolled, bizarre behavior that were said to be manifestations of the Holy Spirit—even when the participants couldn't control themselves. Because I am a person that believes in the gifts of the Holy Spirit, I did not want to hinder or quench anybody that might be having a genuine experience with God. I thought, "Who was I to judge?"

I was asked to read several different books by NAR leaders that defined and promoted their agenda. I am happy to say that I rejected their suggested reading materials, because I felt that all I needed to read was the Bible. Looking back, I believe that if I had not made this decision, I would have been sucked in even deeper, and my confusion and deception may have been permanent. I thank the Lord that in His grace—He protected me in this regard.

I have always enjoyed tactical systems and solving problems, so that when the whole concept of spiritual mapping and "taking back our cities for God" was presented in both a tactical sense and a systematic way, I embraced their ideas, because I wanted to see the unsaved come into the Kingdom of God. Spiritual mapping was part of the meetings. We went out to different spiritually strategic "high places." High places were believed to be the keys to unlocking the powers of the evil one over a region. Again, we were not told about the hidden agenda for the mapping because mapping was done to advance their dominion mandate.

I have come to realize by looking at the Scriptures that God's people do not have to go to **the high places of Satan**; they can simply go to the supreme **high places of God** to break the powers of the enemy, because Christ lives in us. Also, we are able to request that God breaks the enemy's power, because **"IT IS FINISHED!"** through the atoning work of Jesus Christ on the cross and His perfect sacrifice. As I modestly participated in these events of spiritual mapping and conquest, the prick of the Holy Spirit and His love would not let up—no matter how deeply I buried His voice in rousing, flamboyant, experiential "Christianity."

In all these meetings, it felt like a massive group, spiritual and psychological induction into whatever the speakers were saying. There was a tremendous need to agree. If you didn't go along, there was this very strong vibe that there was something wrong with you if you dare to question them. They believed that they were the ones with the ability to interpret the Scriptures by means of their "new revelation"; and for you to resist by interpreting the Scriptures in a traditional way—meant that you were the one who was rebellious, divisive and/or deceived. The atmosphere seemed to change if NAR leaders were questioned about their authority in interpreting their "new revelation" and their tone seemed arrogant and condescending. It had the similar feel of questioning a biology professor as to whether or not Darwin was the true authority on evolution.

I must regretfully admit that I thought that I would never be drawn away from the Word of God and into error. But, for almost a year, **I WAS DECEIVED!** As I wrestled with these things, the conflict of what I was being inducted into and what I knew to be the Word of God, caused me to step back, study the Scriptures, and pray for truth. After doing that, I could sense great confusion in me—a tug of war between the love of man and the love of Truth (Jesus, who is the Truth.) I could feel this confusion hovering over me like a sweet darkness that I could tell was rotting my spiritual teeth. **I ASKED THE LORD TO HELP ME TO COME OUT FROM UNDERNEATH THE SPELL OF THIS ELEGANT, SWEET DECEPTION.** He led me to II Thess. 2:9-12 where it clearly states that if one does not love the truth, he will be deceived in these end days. He also led me to Matthew 24, Luke 21 and Mark 13 where He warns us about deception.

And He reminded me that Paul tells us that this deception would not come from outside the church, but that Satan would rise up with deception from *inside* of the church. My prayer became, "Lord, I do not want to trust my heart or trust any other man's heart; show me Your truth and nothing but the truth."

The Lord answered my prayers and began to remove the confusion that robbed me of my peace. I knew that I needed to go to my former pastor. By this time, he was fully immersed in NAR and became, by their authority, a regional leader and "anointed apostle." It is interesting to note that I didn't know what he was involved in until after I left, because he did not express to me or anyone else in the congregation the larger picture of the movement. I knew he was building networks but I had no idea of the full scope. In fact, nobody at any of these meetings spoke about the New Apostolic Reformation or their unorthodox agenda.

As the scripture tells us to go to your brother in love when confronting him if we have a conflict, my wife and I went together with our questions, and our open Bibles. We asked our pastor about some of the new teachings he was now embracing. We told him that we felt they were wrong and that they did not line up with the Bible. More importantly, we asked **him to show us** how his new beliefs line up with the Bible. The meeting ended amicably without sparring; however, when we got to the car, we realized that he spoke in circles concerning the things that we presented to him. He never answered our questions or showed us the scriptural basis for his erroneous beliefs, which was the main reason why we came to see him. My wife and I felt like we had come underneath something powerful and seductive. The meeting felt like the same spirit we experienced when we were at the NAR meetings. It was like asking a politician a direct question and never getting a straight answer. Needless to say, we left just as confused after the meeting as before, and later we told our pastor that we would not be back.

In conclusion, as a sincere and devoted follower of Christ and His Word for many years, I never would have believed that I would be seduced into error—but that is exactly what happened to me. I have learned the hard way and by His grace that I am fully committed now to His Word and not to any man's heart including my own. I do not trust a human heart because it is *"deceitful above all things and desperately wicked. Who can know it?* Jeremiah 17:9. Also, Satan is more cunning than all men; and in these days, he has many allies in our sin nature and in most of the pleasure-seeking western churches. Through my experience with the New Apostolic Reformation, Jesus' words in Matthew 16:4 have become very real to me—*A wicked and adulterous generation seeks after a sign, and no sign shall be given to it except the sign of Jonah.*

## ANGIE DEETS—United States

I changed churches after my husband died in 2000. He was diagnosed with cancer and died two and a half months later. It was just too hard to keep going to church where he and I attended for so long. A couple invited me to go to church with them. The church was non-denominational and had very different music and service style than I was accustomed to. I made friends with a small group of widows that had a Life Group there which was very comforting.

Shortly after I started going to that church, the leadership "birthed" (as they called it) a new church less than a mile from my home. Cindy Jacobs was involved with the original church; however, after going to see her several times, I felt uncomfortable with her ministry, and I did not return. The original church was more extreme in their actions (people running around the auditorium, people falling out, and more). The new church was calmer and not as extreme in their behavior. Guest "prophets" came to both churches who would give "prophetic words" to the congregants there. They also organized trips to IHOP, but I never went due to my mobility issues.

With my own health issues, losing my husband, and taking care of my parents, I was clinging to my faith to survive. I started noticing statements that seemed unusual to me. I knew that I would not find a church where I would agree with everything, so I ignored practices such as—the need for the spiritual covering of the church and its leaders, prayer walking, and excessive spiritual warfare. I was recruited to teach a Life Group for two years about spiritual warfare. As a leader in the church, I was led to believe that I had to agree with the pastors and not question them. I now know how easy it is to be eased into deception, and how it takes a while to get back on track.

The town in Texas where I lived was very prosperous, and the church started getting involved in the politics there. I helped the pastors and others in the church get elected to the town council and also mayor. At the time, I didn't see anything wrong with one church in the town controlling the local government. I had not heard about dominionism before; and I, unknowingly, helped them to achieve their dominionist agenda.

The pastors at my new church said they were going to "take care of me because I was a widow" (and disabled), and they said it was the church's "responsibility." They helped sell my car; however, after the title was transferred on my parents' car—I didn't receive any more agreed payments (I received a few payments prior to the transfer). They "forgot" and I never pursued it. In 2008, I downsized and bought a smaller house. The pastors were also going to take care of selling my house that my husband and I had owned. They came to me and took over. Initially, it wasn't my request, but I later agreed. (I was taught in my former church not to question "God's anointed")!

The house for sale was next door to where one of the pastors lived. The pastor told me that he would **"sell"** the house to one of the elder's daughters and her family; however, the sale kept being delayed. In addition, while the family was living in the house, the family agreed to pay the taxes and insurance, but the family did not keep the agreed payment arrangement. They also did not pay the utilities, which they also agreed to do. I was paying them, because I didn't have the heart to turn the utilities off with three young children living there.

The pastors kept saying, "Don't worry, we are taking care of you", and "Don't worry, you will get your money." I thought that the senior pastor and I were good friends (in addition to him being my pastor) and **I TRUSTED HIM!** Also I thought the other pastor who had been my neighbor also was a friend to me, and I could trust him as well. Every time they told me they were going to "take care of me," and "not to worry"—**I BELIEVED THEM!**

After my mother died, I told the pastors that they had 45 days to finalize the sale or the family would have to move out. The pastor told me I couldn't make the family move out because, "I would look bad to the church." After that, the pastors wouldn't respond to my e-mails, nor would they answer or return my phone calls.

Consequently, I had to have the family legally evicted. I found the locks on the house had been changed, and I didn't have access to my own house. After the eviction notice was given, I got a phone call from an elder trying to convince me to let the family stay in the house longer, but

I said, "No! Then it kept getting worse! When I finally got into the house, I found it had been torn up. I ended up losing tens of thousands of dollars—not only for what they owed me for the 15 months they lived in the house, but also for all the work and repairs I needed to have done before I could sell it. Of course, after all this transpired, I did leave the church.

I made several attempts to have the pastors look at the house before the contractors worked on it to no avail. After the prompting of two other leaders, my former pastor agreed to meet with me. However, when I (and a friend I brought with me) got there, a different pastor was there who had nothing to do with the situation. He kept repeating himself, saying that "everything was subjective" and I should "forgive and forget and be friends again." This was coming from a man who says that he carries an "anointing for prophetic insight."

I tried to talk to every pastor who told me they "loved me" all those years, and who I thought were my friends. For nine years, I went to their homes, and they had been to mine. Looking back, I believe that it was all a façade! As a result, I went into a deep depression, and I was diagnosed with post- traumatic stress disorder.

I got an attorney to write a letter to try to get some of the money that they owed me. Then the pastors threatened to sue me for slander. After going over the records, my attorney recommended that we not respond and let them sue. I had documentation that everything they were saying was false or not applicable. My attorney said, at that time, we would counter sue them for what they actually owed me, and for more than they were suing me for. I did not hear from the pastors or their attorney again.

In addition, one of my best widow friends was the grandmother of the family who lived in my house. She was someone that I co-led a Life Group with, frequently went out to lunch with, and who I went on vacations with. She told me that the house situation would not affect our friendship. Yet, after a while, she was acting differently toward me, so I went to talk to her, and more about the situation was revealed. She told me that the people living in my house didn't have the credit or the money to buy that house even shortly after they had moved in. So for fifteen months, they all knew I would not get my money. They lied to me and were seeing how long they could use me. She told me that she didn't want to be friends any more but wanted me to "pretend" that everything was fine—for the sake of the Life Group. I refused to pretend anything for anybody. As a result, I left her house that day and have not seen her since. I later learned that she was telling my friends to have nothing to do with me.

I cannot explain how it felt that the people I was involved with were not only my church family but some of my best friends. I was in leadership and attended many leadership functions with them, however, I think that was just another ploy to use me. I wrote to both of the governing "apostles" and the elders of my former church, explaining what happened. The "apostles" would not talk to me. One elder contacted me and gave me conditions under which he would meet with me. It was just more of the same—that the "apostles" were not to be questioned, and that the "apostles" set the rules. A meeting never happened!

I started researching the background of the church—including the pastors, elders, and other people connected there. They had "apostles" and "prophets" who I naively thought were deacons, because I had never gone to a non-denominational church before. The original church states on their web page: *Peter Wagner, former Fuller Seminary professor and now president of Global Harvest Ministries uses the term the "New Apostolic Reformation"—to describe the present worldwide move of God. The New Apostolic Reformation is focused on the Kingdom of God and its King—Jesus. These churches believe in the truth of God's Word, have expressive praise and worship, believe in the gifts and operation of the Holy Spirit, and are committed to advancing His Kingdom.* Strangely, I went to that church for nine years and I never heard the term—*"New Apostolic Reformation" or "NAR."*

**I DIDN'T KNOW EVIL LIKE THIS EXISTED INSIDE A CHURCH!** I doubt I will ever be as trusting as I was before; I've changed! My soul was damaged! But I didn't lose my faith. I went to counseling for a couple of years and joined support groups—and every day I got better!

In addition, I have spent a lot of time reading about the New Apostolic Reformation. As a result, I now pass this information on to as many people as I can; moreover, I share about what happened to me, and also share about others who have been spiritually abused. Some are not interested in hearing—some get angry but a few eventually listen. I tend not to trust pastors, even though a few pastors' writings have helped me recover. 'But before I'll read their words, I check to make sure that the authors are people who speak the truth from the Word of God. It is interesting to note that many that I knew at my former church left and moved on—some have left the church completely, some go to other churches; and, unfortunately, some go to other NAR churches. I have always enjoyed and wanted to help others. I think it is a good thing to tell people about the New Apostolic Reformation so that they won't make the same mistakes I did.

## DAVID CHOINIERE—Guatemala

**What is the G-12 and how it is related to the New Apostolic Reformation.** Carlos Castellanos started the G-12 Movement and is the founder and pastor of the Mission Charismatica Internationale Church in Bogata, Colombia. Castellanos claims that he was inspired to create this discipleship program after receiving a vision from God in 1983 when God told him what He wanted to do with the church in the end times. Since then, his church has grown to 250,000 members. He also patterned the formation of the church after studying with Dr. David Yonggi Cho of South Korea and then adapted it to his own situation in Colombia. A very prominent minister in Central America, Cash Luna, copied the system from Castellanos and renamed it "D12" but they are the same systems.

The chief belief of the G-12 movement is the "government of 12" principle," a pyramid scheme of discipleship and authority. They believe that because Israel had 12 tribes, and Christ had 12 disciples, the Church needs to base their structure on this governmental model and become a cell-church. The model is based on a pastor who trains 12 people as small group leaders called cell group leaders. Each of these leaders then repeats this training with 12 others who then trains 12 others. While there is nothing wrong with this model, their teachings and strong disciplinary measures are serious reasons for concern.

**Castellanos is part of the New Apostolic Reformation.** The G-12, the New Apostolic Reformation, the Restoration Movement and the Replacement Theology Movement (each and every promise of God concerning Israel has been passed to the church when Israel rejected the Messiah) are all flags that fly under the false teaching of the Dominion Mandate. These movements present a false government structure and claim that they have been given a mandate from God, under the leadership of their "apostles" and "prophets", to 1) bring the kingdom of heaven down to earth, 2) establish a one, unified, global church that will transform society, and 3) take dominion over the earth. **They believe that Jesus cannot and will not return until they do**.

Leaders of the G-12 teach the importance of extra-Biblical revelation. Castellanos says that God told him that *from now on you will talk with apostolic authority and fresh anointing. Nations will rise and collapse with the prophetic word that will come out of your mouth.* Also many NAR leaders, such as Cindy Jacobs, attend yearly conferences around the world hosted by Mission Charismatica Internationale Church. The following is a first handed account from a man in Guatemala who began the process of the G-12 group leadership training and his inside perspective on the New Apostolic Reformation:

**David's Testimony**. I remember when I was in a New Apostolic Reformation (NAR) church. It was bad, and I left; but I can also recall many things which attracted me to it. I was in a cell group there, and they were well organized. We did many things as a group—went on outings and had home barbeques, for example. Everything seemed hip, and they seemed not to be encumbered by petty rules which are based on legalism that have nothing to do with producing holiness. This church has elaborate theatrical productions, and many conferences.

On the downside, I sensed a pushiness and a controlling attitude from the leadership. I could not voice my own opinions if they contradicted group doctrine. All the cell groups were set up in a pyramid structure that emanated from the pastor on the top. This structure alienated us from the pastor and made him inaccessible. My concerns were dealt with through the group leaders who ignored any concerns while pretending to want to help. Their teachings were secretive and new techniques were never revealed unless the leaders believed that a person accepted their earlier ones. I found the church cliquish as they rewarded people who were more enthusiastic to NAR doctrines, and they subtly snubbed the people who resisted. There was no room for dissent, not even to question any of the pastor's teachings—**YOU HAD TO ACCEPT EVERYTHING OR LEAVE**—there was no middle ground. I felt like a cog on a wheel and that I was only useful as much as I was willing to carry out their programs. I knew that if I did not carry out their programs as they wanted, I would be reprimanded. (Actually, I left before I got more involved so I avoided some of their direct reprimands. However, I did run into those who got more involved and suffered greatly.)

I'm not saying that all NAR churches operate in the same way, but it is interesting how similar the abuse was that operates in most NAR churches. Also they interpreted the Bible in strange ways yet claimed that they were following New Testament patterns for discipleship (even though I could not see it at all). They claimed that Jesus used these methods of discipline; but that later, these methods were lost—until the NAR "apostles" and "prophets" discovered them again through new "revelation knowledge." It is a fact that the pastor was an extremely gifted speaker which is very common among their leaders. However, much of their charisma is a façade to cover up the authoritarianism that more often prevails. The pastor becomes a "god" to be obeyed at all costs. He is put on a pedestal so he can say "God told me. . .", and the pastor is **NEVER** questioned; it seemed as if he had a hotline to God that was to be envied. I figured out his game and saw that his "God told me. . ." was just a manipulative gimmick—a way to control people and teach us false doctrines. Still, there are many people trapped in these churches who have not yet figured this out. Let's hope God reveals the truth to them.

After being a part of a cell group for a while, I was asked to attend an academy so that I could be a leader in the church. But I discovered that the academy was really their indoctrination into the system. This is where they taught what G12 really was. Until then, I had never heard the term before. It had been kept a secret from me until they decided the moment was ripe. I also discovered that the academy training consisted of several videos and 99% of them were by Cash Luna. At the end of weekly lessons for 6-8 months, there was a test and a diploma, and then we would be qualified to be a leader.

I did not like the inconvenience of attending the academy, but going there gave me the valuable information I needed to understand the system and how it works. The book used in the academy taught that those in the G12 movement were the children of Abraham and no one else. I felt that this doctrine twists the Bible, and I realized that they were expounding a false teaching in believing that.

It became apparent how the system operates. The system went from evangelistic groups to a retreat to an invitation to the academy. No one could be a leader without going through this process which could take up to two years or more. There was a lot of pressure to get people to go to all these activities; and they were always a secret—until they decided when to tell you. I wonder what Jesus would think of this. Jesus never had secrets that he only told the disciples when he decided they were ready. These are the techniques of the cults.

The techniques are based on the theory of the frog in the water. If you put a frog in boiling water, it will jump out but if you put a frog in water at room temperature and slowly bring the water to a boil, the frog will stay in the water until it dies. It does not know that it is supposed to jump out. The techniques of G12 work the same way: If you were told what the system was about and how you would become a slave to it, you would leave that church as fast as you joined it. But if you are told only bits and pieces and never more than what they want you to know, you would probably not object. Plus they put just enough goodies into the program to make it seem interesting. Basically, you do not know what you are getting into when you join the cell groups and begin life in the church. These G12 groups end up forming a huge pyramid with the pastor at the top. Who disciples the pastor? No one! The pastor gets control of the whole church by virtue of his being at the top of the pyramid.

We were expected to be involved in church meetings five times a week. **The church was to take over our lives**; and tithing and other offerings were to be enforced that way. We had to share everything with our leaders—our sins, our aspirations, and our daily problems. We were expected to get our leader's consent on life's decisions. If the group decided that we were troublemakers because we had doubts about the program or questioned it openly, we were told that Satan was talking to us, and that we had to rebuke those thoughts. We were discouraged from reading the Scriptures independently and interpreting them in a way that might contradict the pastor's teachings. Our confessions to our leaders could be made public later—so as to humiliate us and "put us in our place." This way, the leaders could maintain order and we students would be discouraged from questioning the teachings, even though the leaders promised confidentiality.

Leaving the group is difficult because the church and groups become your life and they cut you off from all your other friends outside the system. Leaders could threaten you with the loss of your salvation for leaving; and at the very least, we were told that God would no longer bless us. It was a system of manipulation and control designed to keep us in bondage to the church.

When you were finally made a leader of your own G12 group, great pressure was exerted on you to make your group grow to the maximum number of 12. The groups are not based on love and peace; these are controlling groups where disobedience is punished and everyone is expected to comply with the rules. You must fit into these groups until they take over your life. Fortunately, I got out before it reached this stage, and I learned more on how the system works through web searches and reading testimonies of others who were trapped in these groups until they finally made their brave decision to get out. **THE LONGER YOU ARE IN, THE HARDER IT IS TO LEAVE!**

I never did finish the academy and never explained why to the leaders. I kept my views to myself. I saved myself a lot of pain and hardship by quitting when I did. During the time that I was in the academy, I was also doing web searches on how the program worked. Because they were not telling me the truth, I had to research elsewhere.

## M. BARBARA HANSELL—United States

I spent a large amount of my early life searching for truth and peace with God; however, I did not know that I was searching. After I graduated from high school, I fell into the hippie movement which was peaking at the time. The Beatles' music was my gospel; and, unintentionally, I followed one step behind them—from Eastern religions to New Age. I was initiated into two different Hindu orders, given a Hindu name, and I embraced the teachings of the guru in the ashram which I attended. I was taught there that my spiritual destiny was left up to me. If I meditated long enough and deeply enough, I would keep advancing to the "next levels." I got into Hatha Yoga exercises, contemplative prayer and meditation; and witnessed (but did not participate in) Kundalini Yoga (the serpent power ascending and descending up and down devotees' spines as they shook, jerked, screamed, laughed and went into orgasmic/epileptic-like convulsions after they were touched on the forehead by the guru.) I was told that if I did all these things, then and only then I **might** come back a better person. Although I felt the much appreciated love and acceptance of my new found faith, the thought of coming back to earth as a better person only if I did all the religious things that I was told to do—did not give me much peace or assurance about eternity.

My experiences in Hinduism opened the door to my appetite for the occult. I went from one thrill to the next. If it felt good, I did it. I was seduced and captivated by the supernatural power these experiences contained. I was taught that we all have the potential to activate the "Christ" within. I thought that esoteric, mystical experiences were really cool, and those who didn't think so were either afraid or too narrow-minded to try them. But this, too, eventually left me even more confused and with no peace.

My search then led me to a "church" where there was a large picture of Jesus hanging on the wall. They greeted us cheerfully and sang traditional Christian hymns. But after the announcements, the leader went around to each person in the congregation and proceeded to identify—what dead spirits (departed loved ones) were loitering around us. They emphasized the value of receiving "revelation knowledge" from these deceased relatives. I was fascinated by this assembly of people, because they combined Christianity with several of the New Age practices that I was involved in and was familiar with. It was a mixture! At the same time, I was reading the Bible for the first time and the Holy Spirit was working in my life.

In 1974, I gave birth to a beautiful daughter. We named her Glory. It amazes me to think that we picked the name, Glory, for her because we were not believers at the time. When I came home from an astrology class one night, I discovered that our six week old, beautiful baby girl died in her sleep. The medical professionals determined that she died of SIDS (crib death). Although devastated by the loss, it was the circumstances after her death that caused my husband and me to give our lives to the Lord. We were radically saved! We shut the door to **ALL** the things of our past that brought us death, along with all worldly strivings to find God; and we received our new life in Jesus Christ with open arms. I realized that I had found what I had been searching for all my life. The words, **IT IS FINISHED** became very special to me! I began to understand that the things I had been involved in were the devil's counterfeit. I found the real deal in Christ—God's plan for me and mankind. I have always been so grateful for what Jesus did for me that I have never looked back, never! I never had the want or need to look anywhere else but to Jesus Christ for anything. Or so I thought.

In 1994, I was introduced to the "Toronto Blessing." In light of my background, I was very cautious and questioned whether or not it was really a true move of God, embarking on this new path very prayerfully. One of the first experiences I had was when I was knocked to the floor and couldn't move for several minutes. I literally felt like I was drunk! It brought back memories of my hippie days; but then I suddenly felt guilty when I realized that I was actually comparing those experiences to the Holy Spirit, and I immediately repented.

I regularly heard that I had to keep coming back for more, and more, and I believed it! I spent a lot of spare time going to meetings and conferences to get more of this "anointing" including attending services in Toronto, Canada, several times. I was hooked! I also spent equal amount of time on ministry teams and fire tunnels "releasing the anointing" so that others could partake as well. In addition, I was ordained by a Toronto affiliate local church in 2004. After spending time in various charismatic/Pentecostal churches, we started getting glimpses of things "just not being right" which caused us some concern. We began to search again.

My husband and I started attending a small evangelical church. It wasn't long afterwards that I became active in ministry there—teaching, counseling and shadowing the pastor when invited to various ministerial meetings, conferences, and community functions. I knew that my pastor was establishing networks, but I had no idea of the magnitude or that he was part of a much greater vision that he was not expressing to me or anyone else in our congregation.

I started getting uncomfortable about what I was seeing and hearing especially about the strong emphasis on the demonic such as—spiritual mapping, and Strategic Level Spiritual Warfare; plus strong emphasis on Jewish practices and rituals. For example, I learned that we were planning to have Rosh Chodesh services at our church each month—the celebration of the new moon. Things were changing. I began wondering what these new church activities had to do with the gospel that had been the focus there once before.

From the pulpit, the pastor asked us to read the book, *A Time to Advance* by Chuck Pierce. He told us that it was a must read if we wanted to "move on to the next level" and "to know what God was doing in these appointed times." This book is what really opened my eyes to the deception that believers have been embracing in the body of Christ today. Throughout the book, Pierce describes all the things that we "must" do to prosper and receive the blessings of God. He even makes the statement (p. 147) that we have to *understand the prophetic-redemptive purpose of each tribe in order to go **boldly** before the throne.* I knew that this false statement contradicted Hebrews 4:16 where the Apostle Paul tells us that we can *fearlessly and confidently and **boldly** draw near to the throne of Grace.* I refused to accept the things in Pierce's book because I knew that his book watered down, and added to the finished work of Jesus on the cross.

Also the back of the book contained information that was astrological and New Age in nature. Although Pierce denies it, identical information was taken almost word for word from the *Kaballah*—the Jewish book of mysticism. His book, *A Time to Advance,* reminded me too well of my years as a Hindu where the responsibility was placed on me; and how I must strive to please God, along with all the things that I was told I had to do to get closer to Him—in order to receive His love and blessings. I decided that I was not going back to the bondage of religion or a worldly, New Age belief system again that I left behind many years before, nor was I willing to accept a mixture.

Seeing the deception in Pierce's book caused me to look deeper into what other lies there might be circulating in the body of Christ. It was then that I found **THE NEW APOSTOLIC REFORMATION**. I was astonished to learn that the things that were happening in my church were part of a much bigger movement, and my theology began to shake. I started searching the Bible and realized that my focus had been on **experience** as opposed to the **"simplicity and purity of devotion to Christ"** (2 Corintians 11:3). I saw in I John 2:26-27 that I don't need to continuously be on a treadmill, running here and there trying to get either the next "anointing" or the next "prophetic word"; yet I continue to believe in the supernatural, spiritual gifts of the Holy Spirit. This biblical revelation was extremely freeing to me; and again, I felt a sense of peace like never before. I was grieved, however, to think that thousands of well-meaning believers were falling under the same delusion of the same spirit that influenced me when I was in the New Age. I was shocked that I had been deceived again—**THE FIRST TIME WAS IN THE WORLD, BUT THE SECOND TIME WAS IN THE CHURCH!** I knew I had to talk to my pastor about what I was finding, but I never anticipated the reaction that I got from him and the outcome that ensued.

I believe that it is important and biblical to have the freedom to ask questions to pastors and church leaders without reproach. The Apostle Paul encourages us to be "good Bereans" and to "contend for the faith."

I suddenly found myself momentarily caught between the love I had for my pastor and my church versus my love for the Lord and His truth. I also questioned what my responsibility was to the rest of the congregation. It was out of that love that I asked my pastor these three questions. (1) I asked him if he ever heard of the New Apostolic Reformation. In spite of his close association with prominent NAR leaders, he denied any involvement. In fact, he said he never even heard of it! (2) I asked him if he was a dominionist. He laughed and said that he was not a dominionist, yet I later realized that he partially taught the doctrine in his sermons. (3) I asked him about the purpose of the networks that he was establishing. He told me that "he didn't know what they were for," yet he spent copious amount of hours for many years building these networks. I wondered what he was hiding.

Nine days later, he called me in for a second meeting in which he made accusations not only about my ministry in the church but also began to assassinate my character. I had been counseling men and women—closely ministering to people in his church for four years with no complaints prior to these meetings. I had ministered in my community for over 34 years without incident. Suddenly I was barraged with accusations that were vague, and my accusers were anonymous (with the exception of one).

The meeting turned harsh and hostile. I became an enemy overnight. I felt confused and broken and betrayed! Although I denied all charges—I was tried, judged, convicted, and executed before I entered the meeting. He informed me that there would be a month of more meetings, yet I was immediately stripped of my leadership and all responsibilities in the church. I was informed that my crime was "intimidation" (to a woman in the church) and that he wanted to see if "he and I were still on the same page."

In addition, I learned from a prominent member that the pastor said that he "had something really big on me," and that he was going to unravel it slowly—bit by bit over a period of a month. Things were happening so fast that I became momentarily afraid, because I honestly had no clue what he was talking about, or what he was planning to do. I also learned that the pastor was frantically interrogating other members as to who my friends were, who was attending my Bible classes, and what material I was handing out there. It seemed like there was more going on than met the eye. Emotionally, I felt I could not go through with more of his meetings, and to do so seemed fruitless. My husband and I decided to leave before the month was over—a decision that I came to regret, at the time, because it left so many unanswered questions. Besides, I had never left a church like that before.

A few months later, I began to hear from other pastors and congregants about lies that were being spoken about me in the community. As hard as that was to hear, at the same time, I was challenged by what Paul wrote in Romans 12:28—*If possible, so far as it depends on you, be at peace with ALL men.* I thought I should give my former pastor an opportunity to meet with me face to face instead of talking about me behind my back, although, I was not interested in continuing to attend his church—even if there was a positive outcome. In order to create a safer environment, I arranged for a trained Christian conflict resolution counselor to be present to mediate. The pastor declined. I also told him that if there was any wrongdoing on my part, I was willing to repent. He still refused to meet with me.

Most disheartening, I also learned that he told selected people in his church that they were not to talk to me. Over a period of time, I would see people in the marketplace in tears, saddened to think that they once believed what their pastor said about me. One woman told me that she wanted to see me; but that she would have to do it in secret, because she was not allowed to talk to me. I couldn't help but wonder—is this a church or a cult?

Although coming out of the New Apostolic Reformation was very difficult, I am thankful to The Lord for many things. I thank him that I was able to walk away from my former church, knowing that as far as it depended on me—I did everything I could to make peace with the pastor. I am grateful to the Lord that he gave me the grace to stand up for the truth. It was not easy, and the loss was great for a while, but I would do it again in an instant! I praise The Lord that he is now using what I went through to help others. That is the reason for sharing my testimony. Lastly, I am grateful to the Lord that he has given me back more than I ever dreamed or imagined.

# TRICIA PELL—United States

I was blessed with loving parents and was a very enthusiastic, happy child with a propensity to daydream. My parents felt that as I became an adult, I would make my own choices concerning my faith. After the death of my grandmother when I was about ten years old, I would awake early in the morning, get dressed and walk down to the pond near my home. I would stick my feet in the water and watch the sun come up. As I sat there looking over the water, I would make up songs of thanksgiving and sing to God. All I knew about Him is that He made the world and everything in it. As a teenager, I continued to search for this wonderful God. However, I began looking for Him in all the wrong places. I became fascinated with the secret, esoteric knowledge of the New Age. A friend and I started communicating with evil spirits through a Ouija board, which led me to discover that I was clairvoyant—the power of seeing objects or actions beyond the range of natural vision.

In the spring of 1974, my mother's neighbor invited my mother and me to a ladies' breakfast. I found myself in a room full of lovely tables set for brunch, attended by waitresses dressed to the hilt with floor length aprons. The spirit of love in the room was so strong that I couldn't stand it—so much so that I felt overwhelmed! The loving attention was totally unfamiliar to me, because I never encountered that much love before. All that kept running through my mind was "how can I get out of here?" As we started to eat, the coffee and food helped get my mind off my fear. After they began to sing some songs, several of the ladies started "singing in the spirit." I knew in that moment that it was this Jesus I had been looking for since I was ten years old. I asked Jesus into my life and heart that morning. That was my introduction to Women's Aglow. These wonderful ladies watched over me, taught me the Word of God, and demonstrated what it meant to be a Christian.

My mindset had been tangled up with occult teachings from people such as: Edgar Cayce and Jane Roberts. I read the book, *The New Age Aquarian Gospel* and other writings that added to my very clouded worldview. These practices led me into deep depression and left me feeling helpless and confused. I thank God for these precious women and my relationship with Aglow, because I was encouraged to come out of the occult and its practices, as a result. (Unfortunately, in recent years, Aglow has set aside the Word of God and is moving towards wrong teaching and wrong unbiblical concepts of spiritual warfare, which mirror the workings of the New Apostolic Reformation.) After much repentance and deliverance, I no longer felt like a branch rushing downstream with no hope of escape! However, it took years after I got saved for me to unravel the mindset of the teachings and practices of the New Age.

For the next 15 years, I studied the Bible and went to church with my children. I was building a life of faith and fruitfulness. I managed to avoid or move away from unbiblical practices in the body of Christ such as—the heavy Shepherding Movement, the Word of Faith Movement, and the "Drunk in the Spirit" movement. The latter one did rub off on me, but didn't stick for long.

During the early 90's, I became involved in the ministry of banners and flags that were brought into the church for the purpose of worship. When my husband and I were attending a church in Pennsylvania, we were asked to lead a dance team and make banners and flags for ministry. It was a joy for me to participate in very large parades, plays, and Christian concerts—dancing with flags. My reasoning at the time was that God could use our gifts to call and reach the hearts of the lost. The Lord touched our dance ministry with His presence; as all twenty-one men, women, and children on our team were blessed.

In 1993, our third year of ministry, many of us in the group went to The 700 Club for a worship conference. On the third day of the conference, I was approached by a lady from California. She asked if members of our dance team could minister with her as she sang a song she had written about God and America. We all agreed to put something together for her song. As we stepped up to minister, the auditorium fell silent; and when we finished, everyone in the room was weeping. God was clearly calling his church to pray for America. On the other hand, things at church started getting crazy: <u>inner healing and the Toronto Blessing became the latest craze</u>. My husband and I started to question the teachings we heard at our church that were taken out of biblical context. Also the activities in the youth group moved away from Christian teaching as well. As I look back now, I can see that God was calling me to a deeper work—to understand that America and God's church were falling away from the truth of the Word of God.

To make matters worse, the pastor was not available to us for oversight or help, and he didn't give us the support that we needed. Things became messy. There were members of the team that felt the need to control and usurp the leaders. There was constant turmoil and frustration.

Furthermore, half of the congregation didn't like the dance ministry and half did including the pastor. Yet it seemed as if the members of the leadership were just interested in the biggest and best dance team, which we had been. One Sunday morning just before the church service, the Lord spoke to my heart and said, "Get out of this church, it will burn!" Our family left several weeks later. In all honesty, I was so sorry to lose my friends on the dance team. My husband and I spent much time healing from the pain of being first ignored and then marginalized by the leadership.

A few years later, we were transferred to the Philadelphia area, and life kept moving forward. At the same time that we became grandparents, my father started having heart problems. Caring for my grandson in Pennsylvania and my father in Virginia was a precious time in my life. The Lord was with me, and He was my source of strength and peace! As we settled in our new location, I found new friends some of which had a very different understanding and practice of Christianity. By this time I had been out of the church for 12 years. (I stayed in fellowship and went to church, on occasion, but had a difficult time finding a church I was comfortable joining.) I was not accustomed to the extreme emphasis on angels and spiritual warfare, the demonstrations of being "wild in the spirit" (which seemed normal to my new church friends), and the belief that **DAILY** dreams and visions were the "new way" to hear from God. Also, worship was very different—as the words of the songs were all about "self" and not about Jesus. I was having another brush with another Jesus. A Jesus that was all about **ME AND MY POWER**; a Jesus that is different from the one in the Bible that the apostles wrote about.

It was during this time, I felt led to get involved with a well-known international women's movement. I became close with the president of our local chapter. Within the next year, she became too ill to continue in her position and asked me to step in as president. After I became president, I felt the need to attend national and international conferences. I found myself again encountering unbiblical teachings from very well-known Christian speakers such as: Chuck Pierce, C. Peter Wagner, Jim Goll, and Graham Cooke. I had many questions and very few answers. Once again, I was sensing the secret, esoteric, unbiblical "revelation knowledge" that was invading the church as opposed to the Word of God. After the death of my dear friend (the past president of our chapter), my husband decided to join with our adult children in the Dallas, Texas area. Without a home, we drove west along with all our stuff—the dog, the cat and all of our questions about what was going on in the body of Christ. Two days after arriving in Texas, the Lord helped us buy our new home. Shortly after we moved, I attended a Head of the Year Conference sponsored by Chuck Pierce and Glory of Zion Ministries in the Dallas area. I was very excited to hear what the many well-known speakers had to say. However, by the end of the first day, I was very uncomfortable with what was being taught. On the second day, the conference was taken to a whole new level. During the worship time, many came down to the front of the auditorium carrying baby blankets and proceeded to lie on the floor and suck their thumbs or kick their feet in the air like babies. By this time, I was so shocked and I felt so ashamed before the Lord God Almighty—especially because the leaders, Chuck Pierce and C. Peter Wagner, looked on with approval. At that point, I made my way out of the stage area. There I found encompassed around the auditorium, a circular hallway filled with booths where flags, candles, and books were sold. There was also an opportunity to pay someone to interpret dreams. The Bible tells us in Matthew 10:8 that "freely we have received, freely give"— not charge for it! The atmosphere felt very much like a carnival—so much for my $135 admission fee!

We soon found a church very close to our new home. My husband helped in the parking lot and I participated in the pre-service prayer. One Sunday morning after fasting and praying, the Lord showed me four pillars coming down out of heaven and also the words "protection" and "provision." I didn't give any credence to it until the following Sunday when, the same thing happened again. Now the Lord had my attention! When I came home from church, I started asking Him about the pillars and what they represented. The next day He explained the pillars to me: (1) Jesus—My son's death for the salvation of souls: (2) the Word of God—Old and New Testaments; (3) Worship—extolling Him because His name is above every name; and (4) personal prayer.

Some weeks later, one of the ladies from my Sunday morning prayer group invited me to a ladies' Bible study. The speaker started talking about four pillars coming out of the earth. I thought to myself, "Anything coming out of the earth can't be good!" I continued to ask God to show me what these four pillars were. The answer came the next morning, and you could have knocked me over with a feather! The Lord spoke to my heart to do research on the United Nations.

When I did, I was led to a lengthy, detailed study entitled *The Four Pillars of the United Nations* written by Joan Veon, a Christian businesswoman.

I learned in that study that the four pillars of the United Nation's agenda are—(1) ECOLOGY, (2) ECONOMICS, (3) SOCIAL, and (4) DISARMAMENT/POLITICAL. After studying about the United Nations, I understood that the pillars that were coming out of heaven were by the authority of Almighty God, and are the ones to which we should cling and adhere to. However, the four pillars coming out of the earth was by the hand of man and a system of control and tyranny worldwide—destined to bring in a one world government and a one world church—and are the pillars we are to avoid at all costs. God was clearly warning me about the depth of the spiritual battle that we, as believers, must be in—due to the United Nations' influence on local, state, and federal governments. This information gave me a new wind beneath my wings. **The Lord used these pillars to get my attention as to the deception that was happening—not only in the world but also in the church.** I continued to dig deeper. I learned about Agenda 21 which is now 2030. Next I learned about UNESCO—the agenda intended to change the—schools, church (as we know it), lifestyles, health and mental health all through mandates. I also studied about the United Religions Initiative chartered by the United Nations, Common Core, and the UNESCO's directing all faiths to a one world church. I began to understand the papacy is the vehicle to bring all religions together under a one-world church. In fact, **STUDYING ALL OF THESE UNGODLY ORGANIZATIONS IS WHAT LED ME TO DISCOVER THE NEW APOSTOLIC REFORMATION**, which is the mixing of Dominionism, Gnosticism, and New Age teachings and practices—all of which has been invading the Christian church for over twenty years.

As I continued, I discovered Rick Warren, his *Purpose Driven Life*, and his P.E.A.C.E. Plan (the Emergent Church Movement), and the alignment of the Word of Faith Movement with the Catholic Church. It was becoming very clear to me that the change-agents of the United Nations [known as Non-Governmental Organizations (NGO's)] were all working to undermine sovereign governments, multi-culturalism, and working to remove Jesus and His Word from the hearts and minds of multitudes of people around the world.

In prayer one morning, the Lord showed me that deception in the church today could come into our hearts and minds in predominantly three ways—(1) **PRAYER**— breath prayers, contemplative prayer, reciting mantras and Strategic Level Spiritual Warfare. (2) **PRACTICE**— yoga, walking labyrinths, practicing the silence, taking daily trips to heaven, voicing positive confession, levitating, astral projecting, or grave soaking, (3) **PROJECT**— the Seven Mountains-Mandate, prayer-walking (in order to take dominion over evil spirits), and social justice agendas. I pray you will be led to find the deception in these things for yourself.

After the leadership in my local church that we were attending took the cross out of the sanctuary, insisted that we pray using the 7-Mountain-Mandate, and they invited NAR "leaders" such as: Randy Clark and Lance Walnau to teach on Sunday mornings, we then recognized these unbiblical practices as part of the New Apostolic Reformation, and we decided to leave.

So there you have the story of how God's wisdom kept me safe in the midst of deception. The Lord, indeed, called me "out of darkness into His marvelous light." Praise be to God! I pray you will take a few minutes to ask the Lord about your walk with Him. I pray that as you read Psalm 51, it will touch your life and confirm or convict your heart just as it did mine.

## JOY McCLOUD—United States

In February of 2015, I had been attending a Church of God in Yuma, Arizona. As a child, I was raised in an Assembly of God Church so I had no hesitation at attending a Church of God. At some point I would learn that the pastors formerly had their own non-denominational church teaching—Kingdom Now Doctrine. After a while, a few things were said from the pulpit that gave me some reason to pause. The pastor always preached a very heavy grace message without exception. He would say, "YOU DON'T HAVE TO WAIT FOR HEAVEN, BECAUSE IT'S ALREADY HERE," and other similar statements regarding the Kingdom of Heaven. It made me hesitate a bit but I figured the language was more symbolic than a fact he was stating.

That same month, a video was posted on Facebook by a church member entitled: *A Fresh Look at the End Times*. The teacher on the video is a full-time, traveling evangelist who was scheduled to be at my church a few weeks later. The member encouraged "friends" to view the video so the Holy Spirit could help them discern as to whether or not the video was true. At the start of the video, the pastor of that church introduced the evangelist and spoke of a journey that he (the pastor) had been on that brought him to a "new" place in his beliefs and, also, his end-times doctrine. He hoped that his congregation would listen with an "open mind." As I listened to the evangelist begin his message, I QUICKLY REALIZED THAT SOMETHING WAS TERRIBLY WRONG! To say I was disturbed by what I heard is an understatement!

He began to dismantle what I knew to be fundamental biblical truths. For example, he questioned the rapture telling the congregation, "Well if it happens tonight, I'll be going with you!" Yet later in the same message he said, "If you're prayed up, filled up, and ready to go up—you just may be going up in the wrong crowd!" Also, the evangelist is a preterist in that he teaches that the last days were actually fulfilled during Christ's first coming and the tribulation culminated in the destruction of the temple in 70 A.D. [even though most scholars believe that the Book of Revelation was not written until 90 A.D.]. The pastor speaking on the video spoke at the end of the evangelist's message and explained to his congregation that over the last year, he (the pastor) had either preached 75% of this same material or he had "snuck" it in on them and wished he had done the same with the other 25%. I sat on my sofa listening saying, "No, no, no!" I then went to my computer and typed in the evangelist's name. It was only then that I learned that his beliefs reflected those of the Kingdom Now/New Apostolic Reformation (NAR) and Dominionist Movements.

My first thought was that I must warn my pastors. I thought, "Surely they didn't embrace these unbiblical beliefs!" But they surely did! Over time, I would discover that they had a very long relationship with this evangelist and believed his doctrines. One week before the evangelist came to my church, I attended a Saturday evening service with members of my family. The pastor did not preach that night. Instead the service became a "prophetic" service lead by the pastor's wife. During the service, she conferred a couple to be seers just like John the Revelator." One other incident that evening was quite concerning. A young lady, who attended there, stood up and went into strange jerking movements. Equally concerning was that the pastor's daughter (who was standing on the platform) was trying to get the attention of the young lady, motioning for her to come to the front of the church. When she could not get her attention, she motioned for someone else to guide the young lady down the aisle. She was guided to the front of the church only to continue the vigorous shaking and jerking.

Twice before the evangelist came, my pastor said something to the effect that the evangelist would be sharing some things that were "a little different" so I suspected that I was going to be hearing the same message that I heard on the video weeks earlier. After he came to the church and preached, I knew that my concerns were substantiated. He preached a message openly contrary to the doctrine of the church that I was attending while the pastors encouraged him on. I found it difficult to stay in my seat until the service was over!

The following day I asked the pastor's wife to meet with me to discuss some of my concerns. It seemed to me that she did not appreciate being questioned. She was not forthcoming, but only skirted around the issues that I presented especially the Kingdom Now doctrine. She assured me that she had no idea what the evangelist was going to speak on. She then asked me if that made them guilty by association. I replied, "If that happened in my church, I would have cleared it up immediately." When I asked her about the New Apostolic Reformation, she replied, "I have no idea what that is!"

As our meeting ended, she opined as to why our differences in doctrine meant that I had to leave the church. Over the next few days, there were various Facebook posts and Instant Messages that seemed to indicate to both my husband and me that the pastors, along with another member, were subtly attempting to intimidate me yet smooth over the situation. It seemed almost like a "good cop/bad cop" routine. I told my husband that I felt like I had crossed into the "Twilight Zone." Later in this process, in a response to a question I had texted her, the pastor's wife replied and referred to me as a "pharisee" and told me that "I had a serious emotional problem!" (Her response was because someone else also asked her about whether they were teaching Kingdom Now doctrines. She replied to this person "Not the way Joy McCloud is researching it!")

Initially, my concern with what was happening in my church was not necessarily what my pastors believed or what they were propagating. Rather it was that they were preaching these false beliefs in a denominational church that were unknown and unaccepted by the leaders of our denomination. Over the next couple of weeks, I had been encouraged by a few trusted pastor friends to call the state bishop of my church denomination. However, at the time, my husband did not feel comfortable with me doing that. Instead, we met with both our pastor and his wife. It was obvious to us early on in the meeting that this would not accomplish anything. In fact, the pastor's wife wanted to know, "When will all of this be over?"

When I asked the pastor about his belief in the rapture of the church, he said, "Well I don't really like to get into that but I guess if it happens—my feet will come off the ground, just not sure how high." I knew his answer would not be embraced by the leaders of our denomination. The evangelist alluded to the belief of the "rapture of the wicked," saying he thought the rapture had happened and we had all been left behind." Furthermore, when we questioned our pastor about his Facebook posts about Bill Johnson and the strange things happening at Bethel Church in Redding, CA such as: gold dust and feathers falling in their worship services, he said, "Well what if they are"? He then told me, "YOU HAVE JUST NOT GOTTEN THERE YET," which implied that I was not spiritually mature enough to handle or accept the (erroneous) practices of Bethel Church. My pastors seemed quite accepting of any latest/greatest thing that was going on, irrespective of its extra-biblical nature. It is interesting to note that when I brought up the pastor's wife's denial in our first meeting regarding the New Apostolic Reformation—she now stated that she was "aware" of it.

As a little more time transpired, I received two unsolicited confirmations about what was happening in regard to the contrary Kingdom Now doctrines at my former church. One confirmation came from a former Church of God minister that my sister had known for many years. In a completely unrelated conversation, this former pastor confirmed to my sister that my pastors were involved in the Kingdom Now Doctrine. This same pastor also told my sister and me that he made the former state bishop aware of this fact. He could not understand why my pastors with their opposing doctrine would be chosen to pastor this church. He encouraged me to contact the current state bishop and relay my concerns. After receiving this confirmation, my husband then agreed. It was then that I made contact with the bishop.

After speaking to the bishop for over an hour, he seemed to share my concerns and seemed happy that I called. He also told me that he could do nothing without my filing an official complaint. As a result, on May 13, 2015, I mailed a complaint to the state bishop of the denomination. During that time, I continued to educate myself regarding the New Apostolic Reformation. I also was able to communicate with people who also found themselves in similar situations within their churches—but in some ways, much worse because they had actually bought into these false teachings. I also began to follow the itinerary of the evangelist who had visited my church **months before**. I saw that this evangelist was scheduled to hold services in another church of the same denomination as mine in West Virginia, so I called the state bishop again. He told me that he would inform the West Virginia's state bishop about my concerns regarding the evangelist. I am doubtful that a phone call was ever made in light of the fact that I spoke with the West Virginia bishop myself just recently. He had not heard of this evangelist. He took down his name and also the names of my former pastors and the church I had been attending. He assured me he would deal with the churches in his own area.

Finally, on September 3, 2015, I received a letter from my state bishop. He affirmed his commitment to my pastors, because he believed that they were people of integrity and doctrinal fidelity. He also stated that they had a successful Celebrate Recovery program and a recovery house for women. In addition, the pastors affirmed their beliefs to the state bishop about the rapture of the church (even though their longtime evangelist friend and mentor stood in my church at the time and mocked the rapture and our church being left, as well as several end-times' doctrines such as: the second return of Christ, a literal anti-Christ, the Battle of Armageddon, and the return of the Jews to Israel.) I have recently discovered that my former pastor has been elevated within the denomination to an area overseer which is stunning to me! Also the pastors have now been commissioned by a New Apostolic Reformation "apostle" who aligns himself with "Apostle" Che Ahn, "Prophetess" Cindy Jacobs; and states that he was commissioned by NAR leader, Chuck Pierce.

Shortly afterwards, the same evangelist has been back to teach at my former church. In a video posted by the church, my former pastor spoke of a day, some 25 years ago, that he heard a tape by this same evangelist. He relates how he told his wife "We must get in touch with this guy and learn more." A ministry couple who were commissioned as NAR apostles were also invited to speak. I have come to the realization that my former denomination has become complicit in perpetuating grievous error in the churches on many levels. I remain grieved over the level of deception being taught and I remain hopeful that many there will come to see the truth. I will always be thankful that the video, *A Fresh*

*Look at the End Times*, was posted on Facebook and that I chose to view it when I did. I cannot say with certainty that I would have been in the Sunday night service at my former church when the evangelist preached the same message. I know God used it to get my attention!

Although I was shaken to my very core while coming out of my former church, my faith now remains strong and unshaken. Imagine if you can, attending a Catholic Church only to find out there is some other doctrine being subtly taught. I went to a church believing it was part of a denomination that believed one way, later to find out that other "new" doctrines were being propagated. On three different occasions, I have spoken with individuals at the head offices of my former denomination. All three leaders, without exception, denounced the Kingdom Now and NAR theologies. They stated that the leaders of the denomination, "In no way aligns itself with these teachings," yet they are well aware of its infiltration into many of their churches. In my case, the warnings that I gave seem to have gone unheeded. STILL I WILL CONTINUE TO WARN! My foundation remains secure in my Lord and Savior, Jesus Christ.

Fast forward to 2020. In 2016, the Church of God pastors left, but not before being able to handpick their like-minded successors. So while having the opportunity, the Church of God organization chose to allow the status quo to remain. Prior to the pastors leaving I shared my story along with this book of testimonies with Dr. Tim Hill, who is the General Overseer of the entire Church of God organization in Cleveland, Tn. I made him aware of all those I had spoken with who knew that serious error had been allowed and perpetuated in the Church of God that I had been attending.

Dr. Tim Hill did respond to my letter to him with his prayer for me that "God will exceed all you expect, increase all you invest and accelerate His favor upon you that all Kingdom purposes are fulfilled in your life and ministry." He made no mention at all of the issue at hand. As time has continued, I have been saddened to see the Church of God, as well as so many mainline denominations slide into grievous error and apostasy as they allow the NAR beliefs and practices to infiltrate the denomination— unabated and unchallenged. As I often say, "The more lines blur, the clearer things become." BEWARE and BE AWARE.

*Church of God denomination — sunk*

## JASON SNIDER—United States

My mother was a Christian Science minister which today I've found is neither Christian nor science. This is a false, religious cult that teaches that we control everything with our minds and words— health, sickness, and wealth. Today it's commonly known as "The Secret," or "Law of Attraction." The problem with these teachings is that it often replaces faith (trust in the Lord) by means of a twisted form of *be your own God* (*The Secret* by Rhonda Byrne, page 79). The Bible calls this witchcraft and idolatry. They are serious offenses to God, and they are the purest forms of Satanism.

I was 26 years old when someone finally told me what God's Word says concerning witchcraft (Deuteronomy 18:9-14). Afterwards, whenever I asked the Lord to show me proof of His existence, He did. Any time I needed clarification or encouragement, He would be there, as long as I simply sought Him through my troubles.

For the next ten years, I went to church on Sundays; and, if asked, I would have said that I was Christian. I even believed Jesus was the only way to heaven. Still, I don't believe that I was saved until I picked up God's Word daily and desired to do what it says: That was when my transformation started, and my "fruit" began to change. (Galatians 5:22-23)

In 2006, I got on my knees and fervently asked the Lord to show me the truth. Just then, I found an incredible man of God named Joe Schimmel. He has a discernment ministry called "Good Fight Ministries." I followed a lot of his teachings after meeting this man. I watched videos like "Megiddo 1 & 2," "They Sold Their Souls for Rock and Roll," and "Hollywood Unmasked 1 & 2". The Lord started waking me up to all the lies I was taught since I was very young. I was heavily involved in Alcoholics Anonymous (AA) at the time (a hotbed of New Age religions). Once again, I was being taught all sorts of false, occult jargon. I set aside the AA program for a bit and all the people who were anti-Bible, and I started seeking Him through His Word for myself. That's when miraculous things started to happen! I asked the Lord to show me that He loved me. He did! Every time I asked Him to encourage me, I began to know that His hand was in my discouraging trials—He would specifically show me!

I started drawing very close to a church I now know is part of the Word of Faith/Prosperity Gospel. The place was full of people practicing prophecy—most of which sounded no different than cheap psychic predictions. They all sounded the same—"You're so special;" "You're so wonderful"; "God's doing a mighty work in you"; "You're going to have a great and powerful ministry"; and "You're going to change the world." Blah, blah, blah. The devil can say the same thing to make it seem like confirmation, too, you know. There was always the same pattern. None of the "prophesies" I heard from people claiming to be prophets in the church led back to the gospel of Christ or the repentance of sins. It was all made to puff up an individual—or to exalt one's self higher and higher—more self, less God—not humility and repentance. The essence of **true** prophecy always leads back to God's Word and the Gospel of Jesus Christ. The prophesies I heard in my former church did not! It was all very narcissistic. Someone else wanted to be considered equal to God once: His story doesn't turn out so well... (Isaiah 14:13-15)

I started catching funny sayings like; "We're going to bring heaven down to earth!" I thought to myself, "Wait a minute, that sounds a lot like the Tower of Babel and building a stairway to heaven"! I noticed people practicing Hindu meditation (the practice of clearing your mind of all thought), many of my friends were doing Yoga and invited me to "soakings" which I knew were not good. My biggest concern was that the leadership did nothing about it! They also read from "The Message Bible" at every service—which today I would call a perversion, not a translation.

I started to approach the leadership of the church. I told the assistant pastor that I heard a few things that were dangerous, and then sent him a few links about what I was addressing. One of them can be found at inplainsite.org. [Simply Google search "New Age and The Message."]

**He seemed offended and his responses were shocking!** He told me "He didn't need any help guarding the flock," and "clearly I didn't know about signs and wonders," and "maybe I needed to find a new church!" I lovingly told him I was disappointed with his responses. Next, I approached the Christian psychologist. He had **NO** interest in what I was talking about, and he asked what made it my job to address deception in the church? I told him all of the epistles were written to refute false doctrine. He then said, "Yes, but they were written by **MEN OF INFLUENCE**" (suggesting I had none.)

It was hard to make the full jump to come out of this church. I was still caught up in the emotionalism of the smoke and lasers during worship.

The singers were so talented—some ended up on K-LOVE (you would recognize their names). It was very confusing! I was afraid of making a mistake! It took almost a year to be sure I was supposed to leave. Finally, I was fully funded to go on a mission trip to Israel with another organization (Good Fight Ministries). The devil did not want me to get there. It's hard to describe how I was hit before going. It was like trying to box with ten people all at once; everywhere I turned, I got hit from behind. Thankfully, I did end up going. When I returned, I earnestly sought the Lord and asked Him to show me the truth. As always, He did. Amen!

He showed me the heresies one topic at a time. I began to study the "Word of Faith" movement and their teachings (YouTube is a great resource for this). One important thing I discovered was that the roots of the Word of Faith Movement and Christian Science both go back to the inspiration and teachings of the same person—Phineus Quimby, a $19^{th}$ century hypnotist—who also influenced E. W. Kenyon, Kenneth Hagan, Kenneth Copeland, and many of the Word of Faith teachers still influencing the church today.

I was going to a local church in the Detroit area. They were excited about a well-known speaker, James Goll, who was scheduled to visit. His style was all too familiar and made me feel right at home. As soon as he said the words, **"The New Apostolic Reformation,"** something in my spirit told me that I was supposed to find out more. Strangely, earlier I found a flyer distributed by my home church, listing speakers such as—C. Peter Wagner and Rick Joyner on it. I decided to look up the names of these speakers to see what they were about. Sure enough, I discovered that they were a part of—**The New Apostolic Reformation!** Since then, every time I came to a topic I wanted to know about, the Lord revealed it through His Word, prayer, and searching out the matter. Also, people slowly came along and taught me the skill of studying scriptural context using (exegesis rather than eisegesis).

By the time I came back into town, I was fully aware of the dangers of continuing to attend my former church. It's like the woman (or man) who continues to go back to the same unhealthy relationship. It was like breaking out of a force field. There are powers involved that are extremely difficult to break but **NONE** impossible for our Lord Jesus Christ. Amen!

There are some consistent themes that come with the people caught in the Word of Faith movement. (Let's set aside the wolves who knowingly do evil due to their own lusts for power and greed. They are very much out there, but the majority of the people I knew were more blinded by their own pride.) They have good intentions, and have incredible reputations for outreach and helping others. For instance, I personally heard the head pastor (someone I would consider a very loving man), on multiple occasions, mention from the pulpit that "many pastors tried to meet with him concerning doctrine. In **every** case, he tossed the things that they had to say aside—with no concern for whose doctrine was right.

How can we practice discernment without solid doctrine? **GOD'S WORD IS THE FOUNDATION FOR DISCERNMENT!** Scripture is the first place we should go to "test the spirits." (1 John 4:1)

Secondly, messages and "prophetic words" spoken from a Word of Faith pulpit and their congregations all had this in common: At first they appear to be very encouraging, almost soothing. But there are so many people coming into the church who are **starving** for a real spiritual experience. The more our society turns from God, the more broken people there are **dying** to be encouraged. When you've had severe trauma in your life, hearing these types of messages appear to fill a void one is longing for. Humanity is becoming more and more broken with less and less of God. When we hear these affirmation messages, if we aren't rooted in God's Word, testing what is being said in biblical context, it seemingly warms the soul.

Also the messages are very seductive. They seem to intentionally prey (as in hunt) on the people who believe these lies. Did you know lions have ways to sense the weakest in the herd? They can tell which animals are wounded and weak, or even sick. This is how they hunt. They systematically attack the "low hanging fruit"—the ones they will encounter the least resistance from.

Since leaving my former church, I've had the opportunity to watch people slowly leave. It has not been easy to convince them (about NAR, its deception, and the dangers of remaining in such a church) due to the spirit of pride that is attached to this movement. People rarely are ready to listen to everything at once. I've learned to focus on planting little seeds at a time when given the opportunity, then PRAY, PRAY, PRAY!!!! The most loving thing you can ever do for a person is to pray for them.

God can water those seeds when the time is right. Also, a close friend and I were separated from the church for some time and were able to see more clearly when we came back. The spiritual seduction had time to wear off when we were away, and it seemed to lose its grip over time. It gave the Lord time to minister to us without the distracting lies surrounding and influencing us. I'm only pointing that out, because it was part of our awakening.

I am firmly convinced that this movement will eventually line up with the Catholic Church, the Emergent Church, and all other religions. We will not stop this from happening, but we can do everything possible to wake up the small remnant percentage who seek the truth above all else.

Finally, I want to encourage those who have experienced the real gifts of the Holy Spirit. I want to be clear—I **DO** believe in the spiritual gifts, and I have seen them time and time again. The unfortunate thing is that people run to any form of supernatural experience that comes along without testing the spirits. If you play with fire without precaution, you might get burned! Be careful! Learn how to discern the difference before "operating" in the real gifts of the Holy Spirit.

The leaders and members of the New Apostolic Reformation are becoming extremely politically connected, and eventually will bring persecution to the **true** body of Christ. Be aware of this as you combat this movement, and prepare your family's hearts for tribulation to come. There will be a great falling away when persecution begins. Please don't become one who falls away from the true faith when troubled times come. Be a part of the remnant! A temporary pain is **never** worth eternal punishment. We need to stand strong and "endure to the end." Matthew 24:9-13)

**ALWAYS REMEMBER**—Wrong doctrine leads to wrong beliefs. Wrong beliefs lead to wrong living. Wrong living leads to death.

## SOME SCRIPTURES ON TRUTH AND DECEPTION

*And great and important, we confess, is the hidden truth (the mystic secret) of godliness. He [God] was made visible in human flesh, justified and vindicated in the [Holy] Spirit, was seen by angels, preached among nations, believed on in the world, [and] taken up to glory.* I Timothy 3:16

*Consequently, the one who is coming is in accord with the activity of Satan, with all power and signs and false wonders, and with all the deception of wickedness for those who perish, because they **did not** receive the love of the Truth so as to be saved. For this reason God will send upon them a deluding influence so that they will believe what is false, in order that they all may be judged who did not believe the truth, but took pleasure in wickedness.* II Thess. 2:9-10.

*For the time will come when they will not endure sound doctrine, but wanting to have their ears tickled, they will accumulate for themselves teachers in accordance to their own desires, and will turn away their ears from the truth and will turn aside to myths. But you, be sober in all things, endure hardship, do the work of an evangelist, fulfill your ministry.* II Timothy 4:3-5.

*But false prophets also arose among the people just as there will be false teachers among you who will secretly introduce destructive heresies, even denying the Master who bought them, bringing swift destruction among themselves. Many will follow their sensuality and because of them the way of the truth will be maligned and in their greed, they will exploit you with false words, their judgment from long ago is not idle, and their destruction is not asleep.* II Peter 2:1.

*I am amazed that you are so quickly deserting Him who called you by the grace of Christ, for a different gospel; which is really not another; only there are some who are disturbing you and want to distort the gospel of Christ. But even if we, or an angel from heaven, should preach to you a gospel contrary to what we have preached to you, he is to be accursed! As we have said before, so I say again now, if any man is preaching to you a gospel contrary to what you received, he is to be accursed!* Galatians 1:6-9. **Also:** Matthew 7:19-23; Ezekiel 13; Jeremiah 23; Galatians 4:8-20; Galatians 5:1-5,

Galatians 5:22-23; Matthew 24:4,10,24; Jude; II Cor. 11:3-5;Titus 1:8-9; Romans:16:17-18.

## CONCLUSION.

It is our sincere hope that these true, heart-felt testimonies have been a help to you. Maybe you, too, have experienced the same red flags in your spirit that something was just "not quite right," but you didn't know why. Or maybe you ignored them in order to fit in, because everything else seemed so right.

Maybe you have had a brush with extra-biblical revelation or overbearing, false governmental, self-proclaimed "prophets" or self-appointed "apostles" who have been managing your relationship with God by introducing strange teachings or practices or—

Maybe you feel confused and/or depressed, marginalized, or feel pressured to conform to the vision your pastor has cast for your church— in place of your own walk and leadings of the Lord in your life or—

Maybe your focus has been on seeking the supernatural gifts instead of Christ, have had unbiblical, "spiritual" experiences such as—trips to heaven or decreeing and declaring demons off of buildings and regions or—

Maybe you have been working and praying overtime to have the faith to perform signs and wonders so much so—that you have lost your peace and rest in the Lord or—

Maybe your pastors or leaders of your church are teaching that Jesus of the cross is no longer acceptable in the 21$^{st}$ century and that the Rapture is a ruse; or maybe your pastors are replacing Jesus with acts of social justice, channeling spirits of the New Age; or coaching you to enter into Christ-consciousness to be enlightened; or relying on graves for special anointing.

Maybe you feel overwhelmed and alone, or confused, because you seem to be the only one who seems to be seeing these things? Could it be that Jesus is calling you back to Himself? If you feel a tug on your heart, turn to Him—call out to Him. Like the authors of this booklet did –ask him to show you the truth, and He will help you because He is the Truth. He loves you and wants to give you His peace.

**A Prayer for the Reader.** Heavenly Father, Have mercy upon me according to Your mercy and lovingkindness. Create in me a clean heart, O God, and renew a right, persevering, and steadfast spirit within me. Cast me not away from Your presence and take not Your Holy Spirit from me. Restore to me the joy of Your salvation and give me a willing spirit. Lord Jesus, lead me again in the plain path of your Word (Thy Word is Truth); You have placed it above Your Name. Give me discernment, and train me in the way of patient endurance that You may hide me in the day of trial which is coming to the world. Keep me on the "narrow way" all the days of my life so that I may walk in Your peace and truth forevermore. In Jesus name. Amen. (Taken from Psalm 51; 91; Rev.3:1; Matthew 7:14)

Made in the USA
Coppell, TX
06 January 2023